Knowing you, Knowing them

Understanding and motivating others at work

Justin Collinge

First edition © 2008

Second edition ©2011

Author: Justin Collinge

ISBN: 978-1-4452-4147-0

Acknowledgements

It's a bit of a cliché to talk about your loving spouse in the dedication of your first book. I don't care. I not only acknowledge that I would be a poorer and sadder individual without my wife, but add without the understanding contained in this book our 28 years together would have felt much longer and been less happy and fulfilled! Alison, you are a wonderful person. Thank you for your constant support and love.

So many others have helped along the journey of creating this book. I particularly want to thank my children, Mark, David and Siân for their encouragement and belief in me and for years of putting up with me practicing on them.

The Kaizen team have cajoled and cheered me on. They are an amazing group of people - the like of which I've not met anywhere else. The cartoons were drawn by Graham Shaw (another Kaizenite) - a generous and wonderful human being.

Finally (perhaps still sticking to tradition) I'd like to thank **you** - the reader. I've loved working with so many of you in so many different situations. Your openness and desire to learn is ongoing refreshment for me. I hope that the information in this book gives you insight and brings you the happiness that it has brought me over the last few years.

Justin
(West Sussex, UK)

Contents

Prelude 7

Chapter 1 - Getting Started 11

Phase 1

Chapter 2 - Towards and Away From 35

Chapter 3 - How do we know anything? 53

Chapter 4 - Similarities and Differences 67

Chapter 5 - So what about you? 89

Phase 2

Chapter 6 - Our preferred senses 93

Chapter 7 - Inside or outside thinker 115

Chapter 8 - Detail or overview? 127

Chapter 9 - So what about you? 139

Phase 3

Chapter 10 - Thinking in straight lines 143

Chapter 11 - Do you like doing or watching 155

Chapter 12 - Remembering past events 173

Chapter 13 - So what about you? 183

Chapter 14 - VAK, going deeper 188

Chapter 15 - Filters working together 195

Chapter 16 - Evolution not revolution 203

Chapter 17 - A filter interview 211

Chapter 18 - What next? 221

Prelude

Thank you for picking up this book.

When I learned this material it changed me. I learned a bit more about how I process information. I found the tools to become a better me. I also learned how others make sense of the world and this had an even bigger effect:

> My results at work changed as I began to put these principles into everyday life, using the new knowledge to communicate, inspire and motivate more effectively.

> My relationships became richer as I understood and valued what was important to my friends, my long-suffering wife says that for our marriage it is the most important thing we've ever learned.

The information you're about to read can do the same for you. All you need to do is apply it!

To describe the content of this book it may help to use a metaphor involving sunglasses. I want you to imagine you have got some orange-tinted glasses, with trendy arms. Put them on right now and look around. Immediately everything takes on that orange glow – well except orange things which may become a little grey. You can still see everything I can, nothing's hidden, it's just a different shade. After a very short period of time you start to get used to them and you soon forget that they are even there. Life carries on exactly the same … except you are now seeing it a little differently and because it is now so *normal* you forget that other people may be seeing everything with a slightly different emphasis because they have different coloured lenses.

Now imagine that, after a lifetime of wearing orange-tinted glasses, you were able to take them off and see everything in a new light, literally! And even better than that, you were able to put on someone else's glasses, so that now you can see things as they do. That is what this book aims to do. It will show you how to take the glasses off and introduce you to a fresh way of understanding everything around you. This will give you an insight into who you are and how you come across that might take your breath away. If that wasn't amazing enough we'll take that extra step and seek to see what everything looks like to someone wearing different glasses. This will give you an insight into how your colleagues, line manager, boss, friends and partner process information and the best way to communicate with them without barriers.

There is so much to get your head around that the book is broken up into phases, giving you a chance to try out the techniques and apply them before taking you further. Phase 1 (Chapters 2 - 5) introduces the first three filters. This ends with a chapter that will help you to think through your own particular patterns. You could skip this section but, in our experience, you're much more likely to make good use of the information you're learning if you pause along the way than if you press on to the next step before assimilating this one. Phase 2 (Chapters 6 - 9) does exactly the same for three new filters. The last three filters explored in Phase 3 (Chapters 10 - 13) have a slightly different feel. I especially look forward to walking through those with you.

It's your choice how you read the book; there's no right or wrong way. The one piece of advice is that you don't *just* read it but do the different exercises. It's very easy to read a book like this and find it interesting. That is not why it's been written. Once you start to do the exercises and start to notice your filters it will begin to have an impact. It's like the difference between being told about swimming and beginning to paddle and give it a go.

So what about it, fancy a swim?

Chapter 1

Getting Started

Some examples to get you thinking

We'll call him Ben

Ben is a tall, softly spoken enthusiast. He runs a successful, medium-sized company with the highest trust among the workforce I've seen anywhere. He runs the company with statements like, 'Everyone happy at work'. I instantly liked him and we got on really well. So when we started talking about some work I could do for him it all felt positive. We discussed various options and developed some impressive ideas. Then we hit a problem.

Have you ever been there? Where everything has gone right and is falling into place and then for some unfathomable reason it just doesn't happen? Where despite having all the right ingredients and despite the fact that everyone apparently wants it to succeed, the commitment just doesn't materialise?

Changing this situation and pinning him down was easy for me. All I did was pause, consider what I knew about Ben and change one paragraph in an email so that I appealed to his way of understanding the world. I'll share exactly what I changed later in this chapter. Let me entice you to turn the page by saying that within minutes of sending the email I had Ben on the phone booking me in to do the work we'd danced around for the previous month.

And then there is Sally

Sally is 28 (don't tell her I said so). She's a friendly and ambitious manager. She cares deeply about success and understands that maintaining a great team is the answer to meeting targets. Therefore she puts a lot of effort into building team rapport. She praises where appropriate and 'kicks butt', as she likes to call it, when it's necessary. From an executive perspective she seems an ideal manager with lots of potential. But if you talk to her team you realise everything is not rosy. They find it very hard to put their finger on what's wrong, made even harder by a reassuring sense of loyalty. If pushed they use words like 'bossy' and 'non-empathetic' and then undermine it by saying that they know she cares about them.

Do you know someone like that? Someone who seems to be made of all the right stuff and says and does the right things yet it still isn't quite working and it's hard to say why?

One day I sat with Sally and told her about herself. I told her what she considers important in life and what she considers unimportant and disregards. At first she pulled away, probably feeling a little 'creeped out' by this relative stranger peering into her life. It was a bit like she was uneasy about looking too closely into a mirror in case she didn't like what she saw. Then, as she began to understand the implications of what she was learning, she began to lean in and get excited. I told her not only about her work relationships but also about her personal ones, things that I simply couldn't know. I described her reactions to situations, to different people on her team and showed her what was really happening. And she got it. It suddenly all made sense. She took over and began to tell me why her marriage had failed, why she was so impatient with certain types of people and then the penny really dropped. In a moment of sudden silence she paused and almost whispered, "All I have to do is to understand their filter system and I can motivate, inspire and lead anyone, anywhere!" It was what coach and author Michael Neill calls a 'Level 3 moment'. Not a full of energy, 'Wow, I've got it!' moment. It was a still, almost awesome moment, when something deep inside is realigning and life need never be the same again. I'll tell you what Sally learned in a minute.

And finally we'll just take a glance at Jen

Jen is one of those people who is full of energy, usually with a big smile on her face, keeping an amazing number of balls in the air at the same time. Although she is beginning to consider retirement there is no apparent slowing down. She gets some great results for her organisation and while all her colleagues would say how much she likes and cares about people they then pause and half smile and make some comment about 'bull in a china shop', or 'unstoppable' or 'needs to listen more'.

The truth is that there's just one thing that stops Jen from being the leader she wants to be. Once she really understands this one issue she will become who she's always aspired to be.

And the rest of the organisation will breathe a sigh of relief and be delighted with the new set of results and profitability she will engender.

The truth is that there's just one thing that stops Jen from being the leader she wants to be

If I'm honest, Jen remains a challenge for me. Employees comment with either respect or jealousy that I have such a good relationship with her. Because I know exactly what she needs from me I do have her ear. However, she's a bit cautious when it comes to looking in any mirror and she's yet to have that Level 3 moment. It's not far away, but it hasn't happened yet. In the meantime, with her knowledge and permission, I'm teaching those around her just how to handle her in a way that gets the best results for everyone. It's an exciting journey and one that is at the same time, fun, rewarding, challenging, results-driven and ultimately life-changing.

OK, I'm claiming a lot. Like the medicine men of cowboy films selling snake oil, does it sound a little too good to be true? Most of us have a love/hate relationship with simple sounding answers. We long for easy solutions while at the same time distrusting anything that offers them.

Let me put your mind at ease. What we're about to explore together will feel like taking off a pair of colour tinted sunglasses and seeing a new reality around you. You will begin to notice things that have always been there, obvious, yet because of our ability to filter the world around us we've never noticed them before. It's as easy and simple as that. We'll look at some behaviour together and you'll see it in a new light. Easy! However, learning to use this information and learning to get out of your life-long thinking habits is more of a challenge. More than ten years on from when I first started seeing things differently, I still find myself learning fresh distinctions and new skills on an almost daily basis.

So what is it that we're going to be exploring together?

Half way through the last century, following a series of experiments, it was 'discovered' that we could only pay attention to a small amount of information at a time. It was suggested that we were potentially aware of millions of different impulses arriving through various means into our neuro-system. We can become aware of some of these impulses at any time by directing our consciousness toward them. For example, as you read this page, pause for a moment and, without moving them at all, become aware of your toes. Can you feel them now? Again, with no movement whatsoever, become aware of the muscles around your mouth, or the small sounds in the background, or your elbows, or exactly how your stomach is feeling, or the temperature of the air against the skin of your cheeks. You haven't created something new, all of these impulses were always there, you've just tuned into them … at the cost of something else you were paying attention to!

The theory goes like this; we can only be conscious of around seven things at any one time. That figure can go up or down by two depending on who you are and the emotional state you're currently in but there's not much flexibility beyond the 5-9 figure. So, to make any sense of this sensory bombardment, we've become expert at filtering the world for what we consider important. You're doing it right now. By focussing on these words and giving them your attention you are tuning out of all sorts of other things that you right now consider unimportant. However, a tiny change, like the distant cry of a baby or the squeal of car tyres or the faintest whiff of smoke and you become alert to a changing situation and give something else your attention, temporarily making that more important. This filtering is an essential skill which we can't survive without. Eons ago it gave us the ability to notice the tiny signals that suggested the presence of a waiting predator. These days it enables us, for example, to stop listening to the noise we're constantly surrounded by. Just listen right now and notice how noisy your environment is.

One of the groups taking interest in this sort of filtering of information is a branch of applied psychology called Neuro-Linguistic Programming (NLP). NLP groups the different ways we have of simplifying into three categories.
Deletion (where we completely ignore some information);
Distortion (where we change the information being received to be something more reasonable to us); and
Generalisation (where we group things to make

them easier to think about - e.g. we think of "car" rather than "2003 Ice Blue Ford Focus Ghia estate with the 16 valve engine, part leather seats and cruise control fitting - though actually it was fitted after manufacture because the buyer changed job and started a lot of motorway driving, he got it from a local garage which offered it for ..." It's easy to see why we might want to simply think of "car" isn't it!)

This book explores the different ways we filter information. We'll look at a range of the different 'filters' we all use to simplify the world around us. The magic begins to happen as we start to understand how we, as individuals, filter the world. It picks up more power as we begin to notice how other people filter, especially when we can see how they are similar or different to our filters. The final step, where the deep magic begins, comes when we learn how to adapt our behaviour to suit other people's filters. This is where productivity sky-rockets, lumpy or turbulent relationships become supportive and the whole world becomes a nicer place to journey through. Again, maybe snake oil comes to mind, so let me give a very personal example. I've been happily married for around 20 years (I've been married for 28 years and I'd guess that around 20 of them have been happy!) The day we came across this whole filtering idea and saw how different we were in certain areas; how we made different things important, was the day our marriage became better. Almost overnight those places of recurrent argument smoothed over. Instead of getting irritated we found ourselves laughing. We began valuing things in each other the very things we used to complain about. Without question, my wife would say that the day she learned that I processed information through a 'differences' filter was the day our relationship changed for the better.

NLP calls these filters "meta-programmes". Wikipedia's definition states that these meta-programmes are, *"the more general pervasive habitual patterns commonly used by an individual across a wide range of situations".* The key words here are 'habitual patterns', i.e. our ways of behaving that are predictable and consistent. Rather than the slightly clumsy word 'meta-program', from here on we're going to use the word 'filter', or occasionally 'metafilter', to describe the specific ways we choose to make information important.

That's nearly enough theory for now. My passion is to find things that make a practical difference and so I'm looking forward to getting into the meat of all of this. Before we start, we need to think about one more thing that's really important. What I'm about to say may sound strange but I believe it's a vital part of using this book effectively.

I'm not sure I believe that these filters are 'true'. I'm not convinced that what we're going to explore is entirely backed up by modern neuro-science. Whether it is or not, I certainly do not like anything that seeks to profile people or put them in boxes. My own values say that people are far too complex and wonderful to fit into any box that can be created, no matter how cleverly constructed. Then to go that step further and to put someone in a box and say that this is 'who they are' and that this can't change I believe is most unhelpful. Count Alfred Korzybski (an original thinker in these areas) said, *"When you take a word or a label and stick it on a person you create a primitive form of unsanity."* There are many well-known cognitive style analyses that make these claims and I strongly dislike them for two important reasons. Firstly, because they label people as something less wonderful, a little more mundane, completely predictable and tries to lock them into a certain way of behaving. I think people are too interesting and too brilliant to be so labelled and reducing them to fit a category of *types* or *personalities* just blinds us to the richness of who they can be. Secondly, and more importantly, whether true or not, I have found such arguments ultimately limiting. It is usually not helpful in the long term to lock anyone into any system and make them unable to escape their particular genetics or upbringing or whatever that system is focussing on. As a wise person once said, 'We are fearfully and wonderfully made'. These filters don't tell us who we are so much as how we behave, how we function operationally.

So, if these filters aren't 'true', if they don't give us convenient boxes to put people into, then where's the value? This system is a great model. Like all models it provides a simple way of understanding something complex; it isn't supposed to be true. By working as a model it enables us to work with people in new ways.

Another concern I have about labelling people is that it presupposes that they will behave in the same way regardless of the context. I have found that while certain traits seem to be consistent, others might be very context sensitive (e.g. one thing at work and another at home). So I have a very pragmatic way of handling all of this that I encourage you to develop. It consists of two principles:

(1) Since people are complicated and this is just a model, I hold it very loosely. I see it a bit like trying to hold a butterfly. Squeeze too tightly and it will die. Hold it too loosely and it flies away. If the model seems to fit then I'll use it, and if it doesn't then I'll move on and use something else.

(2) Since people are complicated and this is just a model, I don't fret over what I don't understand. Don't get me wrong, I love exploring the exciting complexity of the human psyche. But for me it's a bit like eating a roast dinner. When I come across a bone I have a choice. I could spend a long, long time trying to pull it apart and grind it down until it's something I could eat (though by then it's probably become something no-one would want to eat). Or I can put it to one side and enjoy the parts of the meal that are digestible. I choose to enjoy the meal rather than feel obliged to pin down every response or comment (to mix my metaphors). This way of

thinking is not only more satisfying, it's actually more useful too.

In summary, what we're about to learn is more like a novel than a rule book. Using our metaphor, we'll take off the tinted glasses and see things that we'd never noticed before. However, don't for a moment believe we're seeing *reality;* we've not reached the bottom, we're just another level deeper that's all.

Now that's clear, I think we're ready. As we start, to give you a sense of the value of what you're about to learn, let's see exactly what happened with Ben, Sally and Jen.

Ben was the hard-to-pin-down Managing Director. What was it that changed his mind-set and made him reach for the phone and book me in?

I've spent a bit of time with Ben and got to know him quite well. He is a very positive, glass-half-full, sort of guy. You'd like him if you met him. He's not got a bad word to say about anyone. And that last sentence actually catches one of his filters perfectly. Ben is motivated more by loss than by gain. ("He's **not got** a **bad** word to say", rather than "He's always **got** something **good** to say"). He feels the pain from not getting something more sharply than he feels pleasure from getting it. In filter terms we call this 'Away From' motivation rather than 'Towards' motivation.

I'd observed this in Ben from general conversation about a range of things. For Ben, his 'Away From' filter was a strong one. As we shall see, each of these filters is a spectrum; we can be at one end or another or sitting happily somewhere in the middle. When we describe a filter as a 'strong' one we're saying that this person is nearer one end of the spectrum. So all I did was write to him using his filter. This is what I wrote:

> *This is an opportunity we mustn't miss. The possible loss of a great developing friendship and working relationship would be a real shame if we don't make it work. The potential money and good will you're losing because of the issues outlined not being dealt with is too important to ignore. Just imagine the fun, satisfaction and further step towards perfection that we won't be creating if we don't do this.*

While I wrote that slightly tongue in cheek, remember it had the immediate effect of moving something on that had got stuck. Notice how everything in that paragraph is about what we'll lose if we don't do it. I had lunch with someone yesterday who wouldn't understand any of that paragraph. She's strongly 'towards'. This is what I would write to her in the same situation:

> *This is a wonderful opportunity. I'm delighted to have the chance to build a great friendship as well as a successful working relationship. Think about the potential benefits, both financial and the good will we'll gain by dealing with the issues we've outlined. Just imagine the fun, satisfaction and further step towards perfection that we'll create as we do this.*

It would be very easy to read this and dismiss the changes as nit-picking. Before you do, did you notice your own reaction to both paragraphs? Did one appeal to you more than the other? Which would I need to write to you? Can you see the possible gains by learning how to do this and the lost opportunity if you miss it? (By the way, that last sentence was designed to catch everyone - Towards and Away From). And it's really not hard to learn these skills and make a real difference to the way you come across, though if you don't put in the practice you'll waste the opportunity being given to you. (OK, I'll stop now).

It's worth recognising that some people don't like this thinking and would prefer that we didn't know this stuff. I occasionally get criticised as being manipulative. I understand that comment. The line between manipulation and better communication can seem a fine one. My personal determination is to be the best communicator I can be. I told Ben all about what I'd done and he loved discovering more about himself, how he operated and, rather than being manipulative, this built trust and openness between us.

Sally was the ambitious manager. A strong filter for Sally is her 'Internal Frame of Reference'. This means that she trusts her own judgement far more than anyone else's. Again we've got a whole chapter about this coming up, with a much more complete description of this filter and its implications. For now let me explain that the key issues for Sally were:

- To realise that she needed to value feedback being given to her;
- That some people needed to be told whether their work was good enough - they didn't already know (that was a big surprise for Sally);
- She was difficult to motivate because she didn't really listen to other people's ideas;

- When she was highly motivated she was a whirlwind blowing everything else over. When de-motivated talking to her was like talking to a brick.

The exciting moment happened when Sally realised that this amazing strength of hers was also a major weakness. All she had to do was learn to see the world through different eyes. It wasn't even that hard, it just took practice.

All it took was to learn the principle, see how to apply it and then practice

Jen was the highly motivated, older senior manager. Jen is a little more complicated. Her strong filter is around 'Difference'. To understand the world around her she tends to mismatch. Tell her something and she'll get her head around it by talking about what it isn't like. This can be very frustrating. It also means that she tends to jump from one subject to another and for a 'Similarities person' there's no way of following the leap. So her team tend to leave her office bewildered, not sure what they've just agreed to. I've worked with a number of her team and taught them how 'Differences' people see the world. The change in relationships and results is tangible. Although Jen has yet to really grasp how powerful it would be for her to learn to filter differently, her team is convinced. And all it took was to learn the principle, see how to apply it and then practice.

This formula, **learn**, **apply** and **practice** is the secret to the almost telepathic abilities you can gain, if you want to. As you learn about the different filters and see yourself in them, they will make an impact straight away. However, to make real use of these 'secrets', you are going to need to study how to apply them. By the very nature of what we're talking about they won't come naturally. We're going to be learning how to filter in a way that's not your normal style and that is going to take practice. I don't promise an easy road but I do promise three things;

- A sense of amazement as you see things that were in front of you all your life but you never noticed;
- Some real fun as you learn ;
- Better and more productive relationships as you learn to be whatever your team and colleagues need you to be.

You may want to stop during each chapter and ask the questions that are posed of yourself. That's great if you do. My advice is to get someone else to ask you the questions - it's quite hard to respond cleanly to your own thinking! If, on the other hand, you want to read on there is a section at the end of the Phase that will take you through the three filters covered and help you to identify your patterns. If you're the sort who likes to carry on reading, then right at the end of the book there's an interview process described that will enable you to discern all of your patterns in one go.

Ready to begin?

We'll start by looking more closely at the Direction Filter...

Phase 1

What motivates us?
(Direction Filter)

How do we know anything?
(Frame of Reference Filter)

Is this the same or different?
(Relationship Filter)

Most of the chapters describing a filter are split into similar themes.

This is how they are laid out.

Introduction

- provides an overview of the filter being considered.

How can you tell?

- this section explains how to work out the filter that someone else uses. It includes a question to ask and what to look out for as the person answers.

Examples

- each filter is illustrated by describing the typical behaviour of a person who has that particular filter. As you read each description you will recognise some of the people around you, at work and elsewhere. You will also recognise various habitual behaviour of your own. These examples finish with suggestions of how to motivate these people, including helpful language to use.

Applying this filter

- the final section of the chapter cites an everyday work situation and explores how you are likely to respond to the challenge described. Again you will recognise both your own common behaviours and that of those around you. This section includes a list of strengths and weaknesses, followed by hints how to avoid some of the common mistakes made.

Finally, there is a chapter at the end of each Phase that will help you to work out your own filters.

Chapter 2
Towards or Away From

Why do some tasks really get you going and others leave you cold?

Why do some people choose do some things straight away and others put things off?

This filter looks at the underlying motivation beneath many of the choices and decisions we make. It focuses on whether we choose something because we want it, or because we don't want to be without it. It shines a light on whether punishment or reward is important to us.

Towards or Away From?

A **Towards** person wants to get something and looks forward to a result. These people tend to be the 'go-getters' and respond well to having the promise of a reward.

An **Away from** person will seek to avoid punishment and wants to get away from something. These people tend to respond well to penalties and consequences.

There is nothing intrinsically better in being a Towards person or intrinsically worse being 'Away From'. It is easy to think that 'Towards' might be better or 'more positive' than 'Away From'. Our culture tends to value positive attitudes above negative ones. However, to put that sort of frame onto this filter is a misunderstanding of how it works. There are many very positive, enthusiastic and optimistic people who have an Away From pattern. It's about motivation rather than disposition. It's about what we make important rather than how we view life.

That's what I want!

All of the filters are equally valuable and it
depends on context as to whether the specific
filter is **helpful** or **unhelpful** (please note the
language - we're still not talking about *better* or
worse). For example, strongly Away From
people have important strengths that can be
easily missed if you are strongly Towards.

Away From people thrive in roles like the
Emergency Services, the medical profession,

Quality Assurance and any role where avoiding mistakes is important. If you filter using the Towards pattern and don't have any Away From in your team then you are at risk of making all sorts of mistakes, ones that simply wouldn't happen if there was a balance.

On the other hand, Towards people tend to be good at finding new markets, sales, motivating others, generating ideas and any role involving taking risks. If you filter using the Away From pattern and don't have any Towards people in the team then you risk missing opportunities and getting bogged down in detail.

Towards or Away From - How can you tell?

Although these filters are all about behaviour, the easiest way to understand what pattern someone is using is through paying close attention to the language they use. Once you learn about these filters, you will begin to hear them all around you all the time. As you start out, by far the easiest way to learn how someone else is filtering is to ask set questions. These questions may seem a little strange to the person you're questioning but they are also quite fun to explore. One word of caution; the way they are phrased is often critical and while you're learning, it is better to use the **exact** words recommended. It is simply too easy to change the wording a little and inadvertently insert your own filter preference.

A good question to work out the Towards/Away from preference of someone is to ask:

What do you look for from a friendship?

If this is a bit personal, it works well with various alternatives like, *'What do you look for from a job? (Or a holiday? Or a car?)* Take care with the 'job' alternative. The answer given might depend on your working relationship with the person. For example, if they report to you they might give you a set of answers they think you want to hear rather than 'real' answers.

Get **three answers** from them. For example the conversation could go like this:

You: *What do you look for from a friendship?*
Them: *I look for loyalty*
You: *What else?*
Them: *Honesty*
You: *Uh huh, and one more?*
Them: *Reliability*

Encourage them to keep going until you have three answers but if they dry up before that, don't worry. If you are unsure, later you can always ask them an alternative question and see how that compares to their previous answers. However, it is important to point out that the filters someone uses may be **context sensitive** - so that the person may filter one way at work and a different way at home.

Follow up question: - this is the important question that is going to give you the filter. The previous question was simply there to give you the information necessary to ask this second question.

Why is (what they said) important to you?

In our example we would need to ask;

Why is loyalty important to you?

It is very important to use *exactly* the same phrase that the person used. Otherwise your own filters may change the results you get. For example it is not the same to say,

Why is being loyal important to you?

It may seem the same to you but it isn't the actual phrase that you got originally and this may affect how the person answers.

The person will answer in one of two ways. They will either say something like;

I like it when I can trust people, then you're able to relax and really enjoy each other's company

This is a classic *Towards* answer, talking about **what they want to get** from loyal friends. *Towards* people tend to use words like: *"want"*, *"like"*, *"enjoy"*, *"love"*, *"gain"*, *"get"* and their body language often includes nodding and pointing.

If they get stuck, encourage them to start with the word *'Because'.* This will encourage the sort of answer you're looking for, rather than some long-winded story they could come out with.

Away From people will talk about **what they don't want** and use words like: *"don't want"*, *"don't like"*, *"don't enjoy"*, *"hate"*, *"scared"*, *"upset"*, *"need"*, *"avoid"* and their body language often includes shaking the head and hand gestures that suggest getting rid of something.

A typical Away From answer could be,

If you can't trust someone then you can't do anything. You're not able to relax. You don't really have a friendship

Listen closely to the answer they give. Sometimes people answer by substituting one word for another similar one. For example when talking about what they look for from a job, one person said to me, *"I look for interest".*

Aghhh!

When asked why that was important to them he answered, *'Because I want variety'.* This is a bit of a 'muddy' answer and so I asked, *'And why is variety important to you?'* He then went on to say how he hated being bored. Ah ha! This is a classic *A way From* answer. Some people suggest asking this sort of stacked question where you question the answer, and then question that answer, and then question THAT answer, until you've done it five times to make sure you've got the *real* filter. I don't usually work this way for two reasons; often it's clear in the first place and digging simply confuses the issue. The second reason is that it tends to get very irritating for people!

Once you have an answer then go on and ask about the next criterion they mentioned:

And why is honesty important to you?
Listen to the answer and then ask:

And so why is reliability important to you?

You will find that sometimes you get really clear answers to these questions and it is very obvious what pattern they use to filter. Other times you will get two leaning one way and a third leaning the other. Remember, some filters will be strong in some and quite weak in others. If this was a spectrum (and I'm convinced it is) then some will be right out at

45

one end or the other of this filter, while others will be somewhere in the middle.

Adrian is a Towards person

- He likes targets
- He likes measuring how far he's got on any given path
- He wants to see milestones on his journey
- He wants to know when he's succeeding
- He likes to think about 'the next thing'
- When planning, he quickly breaks things down into achievable steps
- He tends to be high energy
- He isn't particularly motivated by threats
- He might miss detail that he doesn't consider important
- He might not prepare well for future problems (e.g. reviews may not matter that much to him)
- He might take unnecessary risks because he doesn't really grasp the impact of it going wrong

How to motivate Adrian

Adrian doesn't really *feel* the impact of consequences. So it's not particularly effective to explain what can happen when it goes wrong, when a deadline is missed, when there are minor mistakes.

Channelling energy rather than controlling it is the key

However, he does understand goals and rewards and so it is effective to provide clear steps in a project and offer incentives if the targets are reached.

You will get the best results by releasing him from issues he will see as 'nit picking' and letting him express himself freely. *Channelling* energy rather than *controlling* it is the key.

Allow him to dream and explore new ideas.

Set clear targets and rewards for reaching them. Make it clear how pleased you are when he gets it right and 'dream' with him where possible.

Helpful Towards language:

Adrian, if you can get this piece of work finished by the end of the week you will be able to start the new work next week. I know that (someone important) will be pleased to see the progress being made.
What are you getting on with right now? ... What's your next step? ... How will you start? ... What are you going to get out of finishing this piece of work?

Janet is an Away From woman

- She is motivated by threat of punishment and/or sanctions
- Deadlines are particularly helpful
- She might be quite concerned about detail and good at spotting mistakes
- She is likely to prepare quite well for reviews or tests
- She tends to take the safer route avoiding risks where possible
- She wants to know when she's failing so she can do something about it
- She tends to be lower energy
- She doesn't respond particularly to the concept of rewards and dislikes targets (though targets might be motivational if she is scared that she might not hit them!)

- Janet will tend to be distracted by the need to fix something wrong rather than be able to leave it until later

How to motivate Janet

Janet is very aware of consequences and concerned about what will happen if things go wrong or she doesn't understand something or if she misses a deadline. Setting Janet clear guidelines enables her to steer a course that avoids problems, for example a clearly defined deadline is much more helpful to her than leaving timing open.

When looking at improvement issues it is more helpful to Janet to look at common mistakes than to focus on model answers.

Providing clear rules to follow allows her to work within defined limits where she's likely to be happiest. Beware of setting rules that she can't understand or follow; it is likely to discourage rather than motivate.

> ## She wants to know when she's failing so that she can do something about it

Helpful Away From language:

Janet, if you don't get this piece of work finished you won't be able to start the new work next week. Then you'll have me looking over your shoulder waiting for it.

You don't want to leave this or you'll find you won't be able to do the next bit.

Where do you think this work isn't as good as you could do? ... What could you do to make it less weak? ... What could you leave out?

Applying the Direction Filter

In the example that follows (as for every chapter at this point) we're going to look at a situation from your point of view, as someone involved in a process. We'll explore the impact of the filters from two extremes and show how you may function, the strengths of each pattern and what to watch out for. If you find it more helpful to be slightly removed from the situation and view it as an observer (which is another filter dealt with later on in this book) then simply imagine we're describing someone you know and their response to what's going on.

The situation:

You're sitting in your office with a deadline for a piece of work and you're finding it really hard to be motivated to get it finished. Any excuse to deal with something else takes your attention - an email arrives, the phone rings, someone offers you a coffee and instead of letting them bring it to you, you get up and join them in the kitchen. It's simply not getting done!

If you have a Towards pattern ...

The memo from your line manager reminding you of the consequences of not getting it finished on time somehow just doesn't seem to matter enough. You do know that others are waiting and can't get on without your section. While you care about the others it doesn't give you that urge to finish it off. The email that distracted you was from a colleague who is asking for your opinion about something and you know they're going to appreciate your wisdom! You can't resist the distraction. What can you do?

Reward has much more impact on you than consequence. So try to focus on all the rewards of getting it finished. Set yourself little goals along the way and celebrate in some way when you reach them. For example, have that coffee with a colleague only once you have completed a portion of the document. Or stop to answer the email only as a prize for getting another part done. Rather than focusing on how unmotivated you feel, allow yourself to feel great about small steps. Focus on how good it will be to finish rather than how bad you feel for not finishing it.

If you have an Away From pattern ...

You know how pleased everyone is going to be when you get this finished but somehow it just doesn't seem to make any difference for you. One of your colleagues comes over and reminds you just how much they are looking forward to getting it - and while you know it's important you just can't seem to focus. The memo from your line manager telling you how pleased she will be to see it completed makes little difference. And to make it harder, you just know that unless you answer the email your colleague is going to make a complete mess of things. What can you do?

Consequence has much more impact for you than reward. You are bothered by it going wrong and motivated by avoiding the implications of not getting it finished. So it will help you to focus on the consequences, make them as important as possible. Imagine the impact of failing to meet the deadline, with your colleagues all angry with you because they can't get on, with your line manager disappointed with you and how it will then eat into your weekend, preventing you from getting on with other things. You may find it helpful to set small consequences if you don't get parts finished; e.g. tell yourself that you can't have that coffee until you have completed this section. Notice how bad you are feeling and picture yourself in two hours' time feeling even worse if you don't get on with it right now.

As you read through the last few paragraphs you may have found yourself warming to one style and feeling like the other isn't really going to make any difference for anyone. That is your filters talking - pay attention. That preference is giving you an important message about what you find important. It isn't necessarily saying anything about the 'rightness' or 'better' way of doing something.

What if you have both an 'Adrian' and a 'Janet'
in your team? You will often find yourself
working with a team or group where both
filters need to be accommodated. All you have
to do is say it both ways! Doing this may
appear initially difficult but with a small
amount of practice it can become quite natural.

> If you can get this piece of work finished then
> everyone's going to be delighted, we'll be able to
> get on with the next thing and get away in good
> time for the weekend but if we don't finish it off,
> we're going to get all sorts of hassle from the
> other teams, the next lot of work will start piling
> up and that might have implications for how early
> we're going to get away.

I promise that, once you become smooth saying
it both ways, no-one will ever ask you why
you said it twice. I've often challenged groups
to listen for me doing it and they miss it over
and over again. This is because the Towards
people will hear the first bit and filter out the
second because it's not important to them.
Away From people do the exact opposite. Very
few people notice both Towards and Away
From even when they've been challenged to do
so.

Chapter 3
How do we know anything?

Taking criticism, giving feedback and how you know when something is finished.

How do we recognize something as right or wrong?

How do we know if it's good or bad?

This filter illuminates the process by which we make value judgments. It also helps explain why some people follow rules and others don't.

Internal or External Frame of Reference

An **Internal** frame of reference person makes judgments based on some internal scale. This internal scale may have nothing whatsoever to do with 'reality' (whatever that is). This scale simply provides a way of measuring success & failure, good & bad, right & wrong, necessary & unnecessary. It can be completely divorced from what others think and based solely on some unknown experiences and values.

An **External** frame of reference person makes judgments based on what other people think. It is dependent on the opinions everyone else and measures success and failure by other's reactions. It can be completely divorced from what the individual feels; in fact sometimes the individual feelings are of such little value that they almost don't exist without responses from someone else.

Internal frame people are good at working in environments where they need to find their own motivation and be self-sufficient. They tend to be good at 'going for it' and can make strong group leaders because of their inner conviction about the way forward. But their strength is also their weakness in that they tend not to be good at listening to advice. They can be difficult to motivate, but, when started, they are hard to stop!

Managers often find *internal frame* team members difficult because they are harder to mould. *Internal frame* colleagues also tend to be less concerned about following rules and will happily go outside a rule or instruction if they can justify the need to themselves.

External frame colleagues are good at working in collaborative environments. They respond well to correction and will adjust their work accordingly. They tend to obey the rules. For this reason they tend to be favoured by managers who find them more malleable, though perhaps less inspirational.

Their weakness is that they need feedback to know whether their work is any good. Therefore they don't tend to work well on their own. They are also poor at self-evaluation, with little idea of whether the work they have done is good enough unless provided with a clear standard to measure against.

Internal or External – How can you tell?

Like most of these filters, when you get familiar with this one you will begin noticing it in the way that people behave and talk. While you're learning to spot it, the best way to know the filter someone else is using is to ask a specific question and listen very carefully to the answer.

When working out the Frame of Reference filter ask,

How do you know when you've done a good job?

Listen for whether they talk about themselves or others. If they talk about both themselves and others, the *first* thing they talk about gives a helpful clue. Also watch for whether they point to themselves or broader sweeping gestures indicating others.

Internal Frame of Reference:

Internal Frame of Reference filters are shown by any reference to themselves; *"I just...", "I feel ...", "... inside ..."* Sometimes I've found that strong IFRs don't fully understand the question because 'it's so obvious'. A typical *internal* answer would be:

I just know it. It makes me feel good. I like it

I know what I like

They often point to themselves as they talk, sometimes placing a hand over their heart as they tell you how they feel about it.

External Frame of Reference:

External filters are shown by any reference to other people and their opinions; *"They ...", "My manager ...", "My friends ..."*
A typical *external* answer would be:

> *When my line manager lets me know when it's finished.*

Or,

> *When my colleagues like it.*

Body language often includes hand gestures that indicate someone beyond them, or may point towards an individual if present.

You can also ask a helpful follow up question:

> *Where do you feel that?*

An *Internal Frame of Reference* filter will point to a part of their body (typically their heart or head). An *External Frame of Reference* filter will not understand the question!

Rachel has an internal frame of reference

- She likes working on her own, or in a team if she's in charge
- She knows very clearly when her work is of a good standard or not
- She tends to treat instructions as suggestions and won't really understand what the fuss is about when her behaviour is challenged
- She is quite self-critical and may not take praise particularly well
- If she doesn't like something she's done there is very little that can be done to change her opinion
- If Rachel's proud of something she's done then it can be very hard to help her to see how it could be improved; she would rather spend her energy on something more worthwhile
- Rachel often touts the rules and is impatient with any restrictions she sees as unreasonable, especially the 'little things' like dress code
- Managers may find her difficult and interpret her confidence as arrogance
- Rachel can resent having to do work she doesn't agree with or see as valuable

How to motivate Rachel

Once you understand that Rachel's world is evaluated by an invisible rule, things become much clearer. Since she evaluates the world on her terms it is important to seek to understand those terms. The **only** way to motivate a person with a strong internal frame of reference is to use their own standards. Simply telling them that in your opinion something can be improved, or that the work doesn't measure up to some set of corporate standards doesn't help much. Rachel is equally hard to encourage - telling her that a piece of work is exceptional makes little difference unless she can see it for herself.

The way to motivate her is to seek to guide her as she makes her own decisions and evaluations.

Helpful language:

> Rachel, what do **you** think of this piece of work?
> If you were to improve it what could you do?
> What is best about it? What is weakest? How
> could you make that part stronger?
>
> Why do you think we require this sort of

behaviour? How would it affect you if everyone else broke this rule?

Mark has an external frame of reference

- He needs to have feedback and is a little lost without it
- He finds it hard to stay motivated if he doesn't have a clear set of guidelines to follow
- He tends to take suggestions as instructions
- He works well in a collaborative environment
- He can be a good follower or leaders so long as there is clear feedback and lines of communication
- He tends to follow the rules, but the rules could be ones made by peers.
- He responds well to positive correction, enjoying being able to please his manager
- He may find working alone difficult because he swiftly becomes unsure whether his work is of value or not

He tends to take suggestions as instructions

How to motivate Mark

Once you realise that Mark makes judgements about everything based on feedback he becomes quite easy to motivate. Providing regular information about how he's doing and where he could improve is all he really needs. Reward systems work quite well and feedback from other people can be especially helpful. Since he won't be able to judge whether a piece of work is good enough, he can get de-motivated from working on his own too long.

Mark won't respond particularly well to being asked his opinion and it may be important to teach him techniques to be able to assess his

Everyone says we deliver excellent service

own work. The best way to do this is to provide a clear scheme to measure his work against.

Helpful language:

Anything that refers to his work and gives him a clear idea of what you feel about it.

Remember that he will take suggestions as instructions so be careful about saying off the cuff ideas that you haven't thought through!

Applying the Frame of Reference Filter

As with the Direction filter, we're going to explore the application of this filter by looking at the impact it has on an everyday work situation.

The situation:

You have completed the piece of work required in the previous chapter. You're about to hand it in. What are the possible issues? ...

Internal Frame of Reference

If you use an Internal pattern you may feel two different ways; either satisfied that it's of the standard required and happy to hand it in, or uncomfortable about the quality and really uneasy about handing it in but not sure what else to do. The important fact to be clear about is to understand that although you hold your opinion in high regard, it's not necessarily accurate! You may love what you've done, you may hate it. What is important is whether it is of the standard required, not how you feel about it. Your strength is in being able to get on without constant encouragement and your weakness is that you're not good at valuing what other people say. This means that it may be great and everyone loves it, but unless you feel the same way you are in danger of dismissing their views. Or it may be poor and everyone tries to tell you (gently of course) and you, again, dismiss their views because in the end your opinion is more important to you than theirs.

If you have a strong internal frame of reference then this is the question to be sure to ask of yourself, *"What do **I** think I could change to make this even better?"* If you're going to ask others then decide in advance that, whatever they say, you are going to respond to them 'for their sake' (i.e. it is still every bit as good as you thought but they need a little more because they are not quite as on the ball as you!) Although they may well be wrong, choose to make the changes they suggest to help them with their particular sensitivities.

It will help to remind yourself that your judgement is not necessarily the only valid one and you remember to respond to others' comments you won't go far wrong.

External Frame of Reference

If, on the other hand, you use an External Frame of Reference your problem is that you don't have a strong feeling about the work. You aren't sure whether you like it or not, whether it's good enough or not. You always like to pass it by someone else first and get their response before finally submitting it. That's fine. That's good practice. Just don't allow lots of different points of view to back you into a corner trying to please everyone and ending up with a middle-of-the-road document that pleases no-one. The best answer for you is to find a very small group of people (maybe two?) whose opinion you trust and use them as your sounding board. Make the decision to trust their viewpoint and go with that. Be disciplined about not passing it around to anyone else. One or two responses from people you know will be honest are enough.

Chapter 4

Is this the same or different?

How to deal with someone who always seems to disagree with you (though you might not agree with the solution!)

Relationship Filter

Look at two similar objects. What do you notice? Do you notice what is the same about the objects, or what is different? Which bits do you become aware of first?

Like most of the filters it can be quite surprising to realise just how consistent people are in the way that they notice things. A *'similarities person'* is likely to notice similarities whether they are at work or chatting with friends. And, like most filters, if a person is strongly orientated towards one extreme or another, it is likely to have a huge impact on **all** they do and say. This is because it will affect everything they pay attention to, and that in turn affects how they relate to the world around them.

A Similarities pattern notices links. They see how people, objects and events relate to each other. They perceive their environment as an interconnected web of cause and effect. They tend to be good at understanding systems and people. They like routine and enjoy knowing what's expected. They tend to stay in roles longer since they are comfortable when they know how everything hangs together.

A Differences pattern notices changes. They see small differences. They perceive their environment as a collection of distinctions. They tend to enjoy change and will alter routine just to see what happens - even if the new way of doing something is not as good as the original. This is why they can be terrible at following set procedures. *Differences people* can be seen as argumentative because their way of processing information is to mismatch. To a *Similarities person* that mismatching comes across as either negative or arrogant, possibly believing they think they have something better to say. *Differences people* tend to change roles quite regularly unless they find a role that allows them a great deal of flexibility and variation.

Similarities or Differences?
How can you tell?

The questions we used in the last two chapters usually give reasonably clear answers. Getting an understanding of how people use this filter can be a bit more subtle.

One way of working out the filter is to ask;

> *Compare this year to last year*

As they answer, listen closely for whether they talk about the similarities or the differences between this year and last year. No matter how much has changed, there will be loads of things that are still constant. Or no matter how little has changed; there will still be a load to talk about that's different. Which is it that they focus on?

Typical Similarities answer:

> *I'm still working with the same team in the same office*

A Similarities filter is shown through the use of phrases like; *"alike"*, *"similar"*, *"both"*, *"...they ..."*, *"maintain"*, *"keep"*, *"stays the same"*. Listen out for generalities and a grouping of things together.

Typical Differences answer:

I've moved desk and am now responsible for data collection, last year I was more involved in accounts.

A Differences filter is shown by the use of phrases like; *"different"*, *"that one"*, *"this one"*, *"no relationship"*. They will point out everything that's changed and tend to focus on specifics.

The majority of people tend towards favouring similarities (See Chapter 16 for more details on this). You may also find someone who notice Similarities *first* and then go on to notice Differences. Or they may do the opposite and notice Differences first and then Similarities. A typical *Similarities* **and then** *Differences* answer:

I'm in the same office but now am dealing with data collection

A typical *Differences* **then** *Similarities* answer:

I've moved desks but am still with the same team

I like to get people to talk about objects so often lay two pens side by side and say to them,

Tell me about these two pens

(That phrase is carefully worded; if using this technique I advise you to keep to this phrase). I choose these pens very carefully. They are very alike (e.g. both ball points) rather than completely different (e.g. a felt pen and a biro). I also put them facing roughly the same direction. It's also quite important that the objects chosen (I've also used glasses, books, cruet etc) have no emotional relevance to the person. For example, if you borrow their precious Mont Blanc pen to lay alongside your Papermate it's likely to skew the results somewhat.

A typical **Similarities answer** to *"Tell me about these pens"*

> *They are both pens. You write with them. They both have ink inside. They are sitting on this table, pointing the same way. They're about the same length. They both have clips.*

A typical **Differences answer** to the same question:

That pen has writing on it. One is probably black ink and the other I don't know. I like this one. They are pointing in slightly different directions. That one is longer than the other.

Notice that a Similarities filter sees them as the same length (because they are, *near enough*) and a Differences pattern thinks of them as different lengths. The Similarities pattern notices that they are facing the same way (again they are, *near enough*) and the Differences filter notices the ... well, difference.

I personally have a strong Differences filter and I struggle to understand how anyone could say that these pens are the same length or facing the same way.

For someone with a strong Similarities filter the previous comment will seem petty and nit-picking.

Jenny notices similarities

- Jenny likes routine.
- She likes to know what's going to happen next and isn't particularly fond of surprises.
- She can get disturbed when plans change unexpectedly.

- Jenny can get anxious when uncertain about the future - immediate or distant.
- She enjoys seeing links between things and learns best by making links between something new and what she already knows.
- Jenny is quite good at seeing how people and things relate to each other.
- She responds well to timetables and likes agendas.
- If she follows instructions she will follow them faithfully. She finds comfort in the safety of a known pattern.
- When in employment, Jenny will tend to stay in a job for a number of years before considering moving on.

It's so nice to go to the same place every year

How to motivate Jenny

Because Jenny sees similarities she responds well to having links shown to her. If she's not something well it will help her to understand if you tell her about another time when the same issues were at stake.

Jenny likes routine, so if her work becomes of poorer quality it might be worth checking whether there has been a change to some routine that's important to her. Although there can be moments when she fights against boredom and rebels against the pattern, in the end she will always 'come home' to a safe routine.

She will learn from making links, so you can help her by making links as plain as possible. For example, referring back to earlier situations, talking about how we got where we are, and relating the current situation to anything else all will help Jenny to build up a clear picture in her head. Once that understanding of how it all fits together is clear, Jenny will be much more confident to move forward and her productivity will increase.

Helpful language:

Jenny, the difficulties we're facing in this project are the same sort of thing we overcame in xxx project..

(Even if they feel very different to you it is amazing how *Similarities* people will find those links anyway).

In what ways do you think this is similar to what we learned before?

When have you felt this way before? What is the same about this situation compared to that one?

Jon notices differences

- He sees all the little differences between things, even when they are almost imperceptible to others.
- He notices when things don't match.
- He enjoys change.
- He fights routine, preferring to find his own way rather than follow another. If he has to follow someone else's lead he might change something in small ways.
- He is poor at following instructions, choosing to make it up himself.
- He likes surprises.
- He would rather alter something 'to see what would happen', even if that change is for the worst.
- It may sound like Jon disagrees with anything anyone says.
- Jon is poor at spotting links and so can be out of his depth when expected to see how his behaviour or performance can affect others.
- He might be poor at following timetables and agendas.
- He will change jobs regularly unless given an unpredictable role.

- Jon gets bored quite quickly and will respond well to being given something new to do.

I've been in this job for 12 months now – just right for a change

How to motivate Jon

The secret to motivating Jon is to realise that to understand you he will mismatch whatever is said. Therefore reverse psychology can be quite powerful. Telling him that he will disagree with what you're about to say is an excellent way of getting him to agree with you!

Boredom is quite a big motivation for Jon. He might work poorly simply because he needs variety rather than predictability. He can react to feeling constrained by routines. However, because he can be very sensitive to small differences it can be relatively easy to change his routine. Even very small changes in everyday tasks may be enough to keep him on track. (E.g. moving his chair to a different part of the desk, using a different colour pen, changing the brand of coffee. Insignificant to many, these changes can be enough to keep Jon performing at a high level!)

Helpful language:

"You are not going to agree with me but ..."

> *You're not going to like this but I think you need to finish this piece of work*

> *You remember how we fixed that problem? The same trick isn't going to work. This is going to need something new*

Applying the Similarities/Differences Filter

The situation:

You've done such a good job of the project *(outlined in the previous chapter)* that you've been promoted and are taking over from a leader who was loved by some, less appreciated by others.

Similarities Pattern:

You look closely at how it's been done before and model yourself on that. You know that people don't like change (incidentally, that's your filter showing – some really do) and so you seek to keep things as normal as possible. You won't rock the boat. You will settle in for the first six months before making your mark on things.

This is a great tactic if there has been a great deal of change and you are working with a bruised team of people.

Differences Pattern:

You come in as a 'new broom'. Everything is going to change for the better. The way things were going was fine, but you are determined it's going to be better than 'fine'. The only problem is that you keep finding yourself frustrated by the stuck-in-the-mud team who don't seem to want to improve and constantly refer back to the way things used to be done. If only they were a less resistant bunch your life would be so much easier.

A better way:

This is explored in detail in Chapter 16 but here's a taste of what can be done to keep the team on side during change. Since the majority of the population have a Similarities preference then it's best to start from that place. *'Evolution rather than revolution',* is a good mantra to recite. If you start from a place of Similarities and move on to introduce Differences then you are likely to keep everyone with you.

My predecessor used to do xxxx, and I think that was a good idea. Let's keep that going while adding to it in this way ...

You'll all remember what it was like last time we faced these sorts of issues and I bet you knew they would come around again. Let's build on our experience of the last time and, using those ideas as a starting place, what could we do better?

Remember, it's all about knowing what the people around you need from you, and being flexible enough to include them while still playing to your own strengths. Those who are like you will get everything they need from you being yourself; it's those who are different to you that you need to practice looking after.

Summary for using this filter to encourage your team

Similarities	Differences
Likes routine and so, if productivity dips, look to see if routines have been changed or uncertainty has been increased.	Likes change so create small changes in routine, and encourage them to make small changes.
Make plenty of links between what they are doing/learning now and what's gone before.	Allow to make own choices wherever possible.
Create mini-traditions, timetables and agendas	Plan in small surprises (eg have an unexpected lunch with them)
Find value in their consistency rather than	Find value in their different way of looking

getting frustrated by what you could consider unimaginative or boring!	at things rather than getting frustrated by it!

Chapter 5
So what about you?

Working out your first three filters.

How do you know your own filters?

At the end of each phase we'll pause and explore a little more. These 'What about you?' sections will give you a little more insight into your own set of filters. As mentioned in the Introduction, whilst there is no 'right way' of working through this book most people will find it helpful to stop and consider the impact of each phase before taking on even more information.

Although you can continue on your own, the best way to learn your filters is to ask someone to take you through the questions outlined in each chapter (and summarised in Chapter 17).

Direction filter

Think of a goal you'd like to achieve and write it down. It doesn't need to be very detailed, just a phrase or a word to represent it is enough. It does help to write it down rather than just hold it in your mind.

Now ask yourself *why* that goal is important to you. Write down the first three things that come to mind and start each one with the word *'because'.*

Do it now before you read on.

As you look at your three answers can you see a pattern in terms of Towards or Away From? Did you write reasons that were about what you want or what you want to avoid?

I've just gone through this process and here is what I wrote:

> My goal was a financial target to hit by the end of the year - I simply wrote down the amount
>
> My three reasons for wanting that goal?
> **Because** I don't want to miss the specific advantages that this goal represents for me
> **Because** I'd like to earn a little more than I am at the moment
> **Because** I want to avoid a sense of failure if I don't hit it

In this example the first and last reasons have a clear Away From pattern. The middle one sounds more Towards. If you have a similar mixture it can mean a few things:

- You might be a mixture and not strongly one pattern or the other in the context you chose. However, even with a mixed answer you can usually see a leaning towards one side of the spectrum or the other.
- You might need to think of some more reasons.
- You might have a different pattern hiding behind your phrases. I regularly ask a follow up question to dig down a little deeper. For example, my middle answer sounds Towards in direction. But what if I ask myself why I'd like to earn a little more? The answer is a clear Away From -

  Because I don't like not having quite enough money to do what I want to be able to do.
  It can really help you to ask these sorts of follow up questions. As explained in Chapter 3, I've heard some people recommend you keep asking until you've gone down five levels. (So my next question could be, "Why is *'not having quite enough money to do what I*

*want to be able to do'*important to me?")
When the answer seems fairly clear I
tend to trust the first answer and
remember how irritating it can get to be
badgered by a questioner!

Please remember that this is not *'true'*, it's a
model. It is a black and white snapshot and you
are a colour film! It's not about who you are; it's
about how you behave. This filter is also quite
context sensitive and so may be true about one
particular area of your life and be different in
another area. It's a helpful pointer, that's all.
Also, please remember that there is no intrinsic
benefit of one filter over another. Both are
important and both can provide vital skills. One
is not better than the other. However, most
people tend to feel that their filter is,
underneath all the positive and politically
correct language, better in some way than
another pattern. I think that's quite a healthy
feeling so long as you also acknowledge it to be
completely wrong!

Having done this exercise have you got a
feeling for how you behave when it comes to
the Towards and Away From pattern? If not
then try a different goal and do it again or get

someone to ask you the questions outlined in the Direction Filter (Chapter 2).

Frame of Reference Filter

This tends to be a little easier to work out than the Direction filter. Like all of these it works better if you get someone else to ask you the question, but you can try it yourself. The very best way is to ask the question of yourself **out loud** and answer it **out loud.** If you can't do that because of people around you then it's better to write down your answer than to simply sit and think about it.

Ready? Here's the question; remember to either answer it aloud or write it down:

How do you know when you've done a good job?

For those of you reading on and not doing the exercise I recommend you stop, put the book down and try it. You'll gain much more from it than simply reading on.

Have you done it? Promise?

OK, so what was the **first** answer you gave? Many people give lots of answers and it's quite interesting to note the first thing that came out of your mouth (or flowed from your pen). There are two possible ways of answering; you can either talk about what **other people** think or you can talk about how **you** feel. Which did you say/write first? An answer that refers to what others think suggests an 'External Frame of Reference', and one that refers to what you think/feel shows an 'Internal Frame of Reference'. It might be worth looking back at Chapter 3 to see what each style means in terms of strengths and weaknesses.

Once you've done that let's look at what pattern you use when it comes to the next one, the Similarities/Differences Filter.

Similarities/Differences Filter

To determine where you come regarding the Relationship Filter, write down a list comparing this year to last year. It doesn't matter whether you want to think about this in terms of home life or work. Try to write five things or more.

Done? You should now have a list of things comparing this year to last year.

As you now go back through the list notice whether you have written about things that were similar or things that were different. Did you comment on things that have stayed the same (*eg. "I'm living in the same house."*) or things that changed? (*eg. "I've painted the walls a different colour."*) Did you comment on working in the same office or that you had a new team member? Or did you comment on a mixture of the two? If it was a mixture of similarities and differences which did you talk about **first**? Remember, what comes to mind first is often a good indicator of what's important to you.

There are four options here, did you notice:

- similarities,
- differences,
- similarities first and then differences (Around 65% of adults have this pattern)
- differences and then similarities (Around 20% have this pattern)?

Now you have some idea of whether your pattern is similarities or differences orientated it might be worth looking back at Chapter 4 to see where your strengths and weaknesses might lie.

Phase 2
The second set of filters:

Filtering information through our preferred senses

Inside/Outside Thinker

Chunk Size Filter

Chapter 6
Filtering information through our preferred senses

As you read this chapter and **see** (visual) how to apply it you're going to like **the sound** (auditory) of how it may help you **get to grips (kinaesthetic)** with all sorts of current problems.

We all have a preferred way of remembering sensory information. Most of us will reference memories through **visual stimuli** (what we saw), **auditory stimuli** (what we heard and said) or **kinaesthetic stimuli** (what we felt or did). There is a fourth common representational system called 'auditory digital' which will be dealt with later since it includes a mixture of the others.

According to surveys around 50% of the population are principally visual thinkers, 30% kinaesthetic and 20% auditory. These figures are suspiciously rounded; please take them with the same pinch of salt that I do!

There is no question that the most efficient way of storing information is to do so visually. However, non-visual people will still tend to use non-visual cues to remember visual information. For example you may remember the feel (or perhaps smell) of a car you once owned before you can remember what it looked like.

All studies done in this area (and there have been many) have shown the same results. Everyone learns best in a mixed environment i.e. a learning environment that has a good mix of Visual, Auditory and Kinaesthetic (VAK) stimuli. If an experience includes each of the areas then everyone will remember it better. This means that a totally visual learning experience is not the best for a strong visual learner! A mixed environment is needed.

There is often a great deal of emphasis on the value of knowing about VAK for learning. What is often missed is how helpful this knowledge is for improving all types of communication, not just learning environments.

The real key to success in using this is two-fold. It is so helpful to discover how your colleague/boss/client is filtering information and be able to communicate effectively with them. And it is essential to discern your own natural tendencies otherwise you will automatically favour your strengths, which are not necessarily the strengths of those you want to communicate with. Your style will support someone with the same strengths as you but may be quite limiting for those who are different.

All the other filters work by asking questions and *listening closely* to the answers. This one's different. This time initially you need to *watch closely*. We give away how we're thinking by the way we move our eyes. This might sound strange at first but as you watch for results it will become very obvious. The first time I came across this I was very sceptical. Then I asked some people some questions and was amazed by the responses I saw - people really are consistent in the way that they look when they access information.

However, I must add a health warning to this. Rigorous testing is yet to prove this holds any water. Maybe it's just an interesting phenomenon that is yet to be understood. Maybe people are so incredibly complicated that this is a simplification too far. My way of handling this is the same as it is for all the filters; it's just a model; it's not a fact. So if it seems to be helpful with an individual work with it, otherwise try something else! Remember holding that butterfly?

VAK – How can we tell?

Any question that makes someone remember a past event will work, though it's worth being careful to avoid questions that have very strong emotions linked to them (like births, deaths and weddings).

Eg. "Tell me about last Christmas." Or,

"Tell me about your last holiday." Or,

"Tell me about last weekend".

If you don't see clear eye movement and they simply stay looking at you then the answer is too available to them and they didn't have to go inside and think about it. A helpful response to this is to make the question harder - e.g. *"Tell me about the weekend before last"* or *"Tell me about last Christmas eve"*

As the person accesses their memories they tend to look in certain directions.

Looking upwards, or going out of focus into the distance, suggests that they are remembering information primarily through a visual cue - i.e. they make a picture in their minds **(Visual)**.

Looking sideways suggests that they are remembering information primarily through sounds **(Auditory)**.

Looking downwards suggests that they are remembering information primarily through feelings and/or actions **(Kinaesthetic)**.

See the diagram below for help with this. For the moment don't worry too much about whether they look off to the left or to the right. The left/right direction and some of the more complex eye movements you might encounter are explored in Chapter 14.

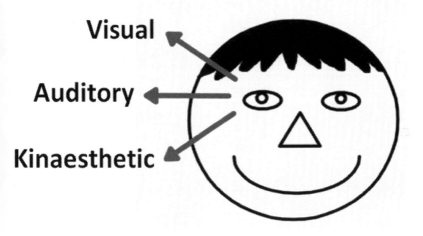

As well as the eye patterns, there are various other things to look at and consider. The way someone is sitting, how they are dressed, how they talk and even the shoes they're wearing all, give further clues as to their VAK preferences.

Visual	Kinaesthetic
Dress smart	Dress comfortably
Look 'smart' - e.g. combed hair, well-ironed clothes, cares about how they look including making sure they wear matching colours	Can look a bit scruffy - e.g. hair need not be well brushed, shirt untucked, don't really care about how they look including wearing colours don't really work together
Sit up straight	Slouch as they sit
Talk faster and higher - with few pauses	Talk slower and deeper - with pauses marked by noises like 'err'
Look at the footwear; it often gives it away. Visual people can wear incredible shoes which must be very uncomfortable but look amazing.	Kinaesthetic people are more likely to wear shoes that are well worn in and look 'comfortable'. They'll wear trainers if the situation allows for it.

Before you write to me telling me that the kinaesthetic column is describing any typical teenager let me encourage you to look at the teenager in context - i.e. with their peers. It becomes very obvious when you have a group to compare an individual with. Although they may all be dressed casually when you look closely it becomes clear who cares about how they look and who doesn't. I was teaching a group of GCSE students some revision skills recently and as they walked in I could see some clearly visual and some clearly kinaesthetic individuals by comparing them with the norm within the class. This was soon backed up by seeing how they sat - straighter than average or more slouched than average.

Auditory people can be a mix of both of these but give themselves away immediately they speak. They - will - enunciate - every - word - quite - clearly - to - make - sure - it's - heard - correctly. They talk a bit like they are a radio announcer telling everyone what is going on. A good friend of mine who is very Auditory visited my home a little while back and when the phone rang announced clearly to everyone, 'THAT WILL BE THE PHONE'. Of course it was the phone, it was **my** phone! His way of processing the information was to announce it.

Auditory digital people can show any of these signs. They tend to talk about things 'making sense' and prefer things that are ordered. The key trait is the power of their internal dialogue. Please note, everyone has an internal dialogue; it's just that Auditory Digital people listen to it more closely. So ask them what they're saying to themselves right now and watch how easily they answer the question.

Andy is a visual thinker

- He tends to dress well and cares about the way he looks - e.g. he will care if his hair is messy, if his clothes are dirty.
- Andy sits up fairly straight in his chair.
- He talks reasonably fast and at a high pitch.
- He breathes from high up in his chest
- Andy uses language based around how things *look*.
  "I see that"
  "I like the look of them"
  "Picture this ..."
  "Focus in ..."
  "It appears that ..."
  "Imagine that ..."
- Colours are important to Andy;
- Andy might show some skills at drawing or painting or photography. He will be good at *seeing* subtleties that may escape others, e.g. small colour changes.

How to motivate Andy

It will **really** help you to know which pattern you prefer. If you are the same as the child you want to motivate then there is no problem. It's when you are different that it becomes important. Remember, we all like people who are like us. So the more you can *appear* like Andy the easier it is for him to respond positively to you.

For each of the filters, part of the secret to motivation lies in using **their** metaphors, pictures and language rather than your own. You can literally 'speak their language', i.e. use the very same words and phrases that they do. For Andy it will be phrases like:

> *"Let's **look** at this more **closely**".*
> *Use your **imagination** to **picture** it as though it was finished – what does it **look** like?"*

Andy is likely to be quite affected by how his surroundings look. An untidy environment can be a constant distraction. While clashing colours may bother him, bright pictures and posters may inspire. A rather unusual survey done in the 90s suggested that any information put above eye level (i.e. above his eyes when he's sitting down) is twice as likely to be remembered than information he looks down to access. So putting inspiring quotes or current information that he needs to be aware of above eye level will be significantly helpful for him. (Please note this is true for *everyone*, not just visual people!)

Information put above eye level is twice as likely to be remembered

Vicki is an auditory thinker

- She tends to sit with her head to one side.
- She can appear not to be listening because she doesn't necessarily look at you when you're talking to her.
- She is sensitive to noise and might be quite bothered by things others don't notice - e.g. the hum of a fan.
- She is quite distracted by others talking or by the TV.
- She may like music and sometimes uses it to cover up other distracting noises.
- She tends to talk loudly and clearly

- The words you use and she uses can be of great importance to her
- Vicki uses language based around how things sound:

I like the sound of that
Listen, I've got something important to say
That rings a bell
I hear you ...
I'm all ears
... tune in/tune out ...

How to motivate Vicki

Like Andy, Vicki will respond more positively to suggestions posed using her preferred language.

I have to say that I like the way you've listened to me, and I know that what I've said rings a bell with you. It sounds to me like you're doing all the right things and I look forward to hearing you tell me about it next time we're together.

Vicki is unlikely to make progress in an issue without the chance to talk it through or at least write about it (she'll say the words in her head as she writes). Be aware of her needs for noise or silence. Some auditory people find comfort in bustle around them; some need it quiet to be able to think.

Jack is a kinaesthetic thinker

- Jack doesn't worry too much about how he looks. He might appear scruffy because he is more concerned about comfort than appearance.
- He tends to sit comfortably and may appear to be slouching.
- Jack talks slowly, with a deeper tone and uses 'thinking noises' - "um…", "urr…", "hmm…"
- Like his speech his movements are deliberate.
- He breathes from lower in his chest.
- Jack may be good at practical things, good with his hands and may like sports.
- Jack is quite affectionate and isn't shy about responding physically.
- Jack uses language based around how things feel:
  "I like the feel of that"
  "I can't get a grip on that"
  "It slips through my fingers"
  "… make contact …"
  "… tap into …"
  "…in touch…"

How to motivate Jack

Reflect back the language he uses, preferably in the same tone and pitch.

> *Now you've **got hold** this, just think how you'll **feel** having **done** the right thing.*

Be aware that how he's feeling about something is going to be more important than how it looks. For example, if he's feeling demotivated then encouraging him to tidy his room is unlikely to make him feel different, whereas giving him a more comfortable chair is. Sitting down and having a one-to-one understanding chat is much less likely to do him any good than getting out for a brisk walk to talk it through.

Auditory Digital

There is a fourth filter some use. This is where a person keeps a running commentary inside their head. It's a bit like an auditory pattern but, instead of needing it to be actual sound, they are telling themselves what to think all the time.

Steve is an Auditory Digital thinker

Auditory digital thinkers can be a mixture of visual, auditory and kinaesthetic and so may appear to be one or another at different times. The thing to remember is that there is a conversation going on inside his head that no-one else has access to.

- Steve tends to be quiet in meetings. He doesn't tend to process his thoughts externally because he's talking to himself inside.
- He might come back to you later on after the meeting has finished, sharing his insights.
- Steve likes logical steps and is happiest when he breaks things into clear sections or patterns.
- Steve may have a really great internal dialogue - constantly encouraging himself and pushing him on. Or he may be constantly undermining himself - telling himself that he's not good enough or reminding himself of how badly he did last time. Because this all happens internally, it is not easy to tell that it's going on. However, if he has a poor internal dialogue he will be 'beating himself up' every chance that he gets (i.e. all the time).
- Because of the internal conversation, it is not always easy to tell how Steve has got to a

certain point. Sometimes he's talked it all through at length - just not with you!

How to Motivate Steve

Always remember that when Steve responds he's already discussed it internally. This means that it's not easy to get straightforward answers and sometimes it's worth taking the extra effort to discern how he's feeling behind the answers he initially gives.

Language that will help:
logical, process, know, makes sense, decide – plus a mixture of all the other language from the other VAK filters.

> e.g. *'Steve, having had the chance to think about this can you tell that it makes sense to decide to proceed in this logical sequence from here.'*

Applying the VAK filter

Your VAK preference allows you to do all sorts of things well, while stopping you from being good at others. The secret is doing what you do well while finding a way of getting someone else to do the things you do badly!

The situation:

Back in the office you're working on a project and not feeling inspired (actually it's the very same project described in Chapter 3). You look at the messy desk around you, full of bits of paper with various ideas scribbled on them. You know there's a deadline approaching and are not sure what to do.

Visual pattern:

As someone who favours a visual pattern you are often inspired by what you see, either by what is actually in front of your eyes or by how you are picturing it internally. If you're feeling stuck or uninspired change what you're looking at!

First, tidy up the desk. Give yourself a visually pleasing environment to work in.

Second, give yourself some colour. Perhaps change the colour pen you are writing with, or the colour paper you're writing on. What if you were to change the screen from black text on a white screen to something a bit more interesting - e.g. white text on a dark blue screen? How does that feel? Or yellow on a black screen? Is that any better or does it distract you? Maybe you need to try something more subtle like changing the white background to a pale yellow. How does that feel?

Third, create a mind map (spider diagram, concept map, tree diagram etc) showing clearly where you've got to and then begin to split the rest of the work into different 'branches' using colours, text and pictures to show what needs to be done.

Fourth, STOP! Close your eyes for a moment and picture the whole project completed. What does it look like? Can you see it all finished? Imagine your manager responding to you as you give him the completed article and see yourself sitting there delighted to have finished. Fix that in your mind's eye. Now visualise the steps that need to be completed to get you there.

Fifth, if you're still not feeling like getting on change your point of view in a very literal sense - sit somewhere different for a while. Maybe even just changing place around your desk will make a difference. Maybe going and working in the canteen/pub/coffee bar might help re-start your imagination.

Auditory Pattern:

As someone who favours an auditory pattern you are more inspired by how something sounds to you, perhaps by what you are actually listening to or maybe by that internal soundtrack running inside. So if you're stuck, change the track you're listening to!

First, find someone to talk to. If you are on your own start telling your goldfish or dog all about where you've got to and why you are currently stuck. Sometimes all it takes is to verbalise it and you discover the answers for yourself.

Second, if you haven't got the answer from the first step then tell someone what the issue is and get them to repeat it back to you. Notice the answers welling up inside as you engage in dialogue with them.

Third, find a way of recording the way forward rather than having to write it –

Windows and Macs are very good at voice-to-text recognition these days.

Fourth, change the background noises. When you do this, be very alert to the effect the different changes have on you. For example, you might like certain types of music but find they distract you when playing in the background. It may be you need to find somewhere else to sit for a while where the noises are more complimentary to your thought processes. Research shows that ALL background noise distracts from thinking processes. However, sometimes the rewards outweigh the distraction. For example if you find you can sit and work for twice as long if there's music on than if you are in silence it may be worth the distraction that the music is causing. Perhaps soft music stops you from listening to the discussion going on across the room. There is some evidence that instrumental music is less distracting than that with vocals.

Kinaesthetic Pattern:

As someone who favours a kinaesthetic pattern you are inspired by how you feel and what you do. So if you're feeling stuck then change what you're doing and how you're feeling!

Have you noticed that this isn't rocket science? Someone once called Tony Robbins, the American motivation guru, "The Master of the Bleedin' Obvious". They meant it as an insult but actually it's often the obvious that we've missed and need to get back to. Most of these filters are actually very obvious when you stop and think about them. This is the beauty of it. All this book is seeking to do is to help you do just that - stop and think about them!

First, you can change how you feel by changing your physiology, so move! Any movement you make will help you feel different about things. Maybe take a walk to think things through before continuing, or go and make that coffee you fancy, or just have a good stretch. Could you go and work somewhere else for a while - perhaps a cafeteria or use someone else's office?

Second, we can also change how we feel by changing our focus. Notice how you have been thinking about a project and list as many ways as you can of continuing from here with a different feel - for example you could write the next section from a different perspective (it might need editing later!), or you could imagine you were five years in the future looking back and describing the project to someone. What if you were to ascribe different positive emotions to the different sections of the project and seek to feel that way when working on each section? For example, the beginning section could feel *exciting,* the middle section, *confident* and the end *reflective.*

Third, you will find that *doing something* will help you make a fresh start. You could take those bits of paper all over your desk and start creating groups, or connections between them. Perhaps you could make a mind map out of them. Move them around your desk into different arrangements until you hit one that feels best. You could change other things, like from typing to writing (or vice versa). You could change computer or pen.

Fourth, if you're still stuck, DO something different. Don't carry on just trying harder hoping to find some inspiration. Find some way of continuing the work in a different mode. For example you could swap from dealing with details to looking at the overall picture (or vice versa).

Chapter 7
Inside or Outside thinker?

Do we process information quietly inside or more noisily outside? And why talking to your dog may be a good thing.

Most of us have a clear preference for how we like to think about things. We either like to do so by internally processing it, pondering the alternatives, spending time alone, working it out until we know what we think and then we're ready to share

Hmm - I really need some time to reflect on all of this

. Others need to think externally - they almost need to see and hear it outside of their own brain before they know what they think. Everyone tends to want to do both; the interesting part to notice is what they want/need to do **first**.

Inside Thinkers tend to 'go inside' and think about things before they are ready to talk about them. They will need some space and can get tetchy if asked to give an opinion about something before they've had that inner time. If challenged they need time to reflect on what they've done before they are in a position to talk about it sensibly. You can often see *Inside Thinkers* lose focus as they go inside. They stop looking at you and look away, their faces going flat as they stop responding. They can be frustrating for some because they don't react fast enough.

Outside Thinkers tend to think externally. They often don't know what they think until they've said it and have had the chance to hear what it sounds like. They can get frustrated if required to think about something rather than talk about it. If asked to 'sit there and think about the issues at hand' they actually can't! They will often just fidget.

Inside Thinkers find outside thinkers frustrating because they talk before thinking it through, they don't give enough space to process an issue and often seem to make decisions without enough thought. *Outside Thinkers* find *'insiders'* difficult because they won't communicate, they seem unwilling to just talk about things.

Inside or Outside Thinker – How can you tell?

A good question to ask to discern this filter is,

> *When you've got an important decision to make do you prefer to think about it first or do you talk it through with someone straight away?*

The thing to listen out for is which they want to do **first**.

Inside Thinker:

An Inside Thinker will want to have space before they are ready to talk about it. Therefore a typical *Inside* answer is;

Well, I like to stop and think things through a little before I'm ready to discuss it with others.

Having asked the question watch closely for the immediate reaction it causes. Usually *Inside* pattern people will pause to consider the question (process it inside!) before giving an answer.

Outside Thinker:

An Outside Thinker will want to have someone to talk to from the beginning. They will put off thinking about it until they get that opportunity. A typical *Outside* answer is,

Well, it's nice to explore other people's experiences before getting too far down the road. And I do find that by chatting things through with others it helps me to work out what I'm thinking about it myself.

Again, watch closely and you may notice that they explore the question with you rather than pause to consider it - that is Outside Thinking happening in front of your eyes!

Supporting questions:

Occasionally people find it hard to think of what they do. It may help to ask them to talk about something they have already decided and work through how they made that decision. Helpful pointers can be heard in the answer to the questions like the following ones (in these examples a positive answer suggests an *Outside* pattern)

"Do you find it helps to talk about issues you're facing?"

"Do you sometimes find yourself answering your own question when chatting?"

"Do you sometimes talk to yourself?"

"Do you ever start a sentence with phases like, 'I'm not entirely sure what I'm saying here but...' ?"

Jason is an outside thinker

- Jason has a need to talk about everything.
- He doesn't know what he is thinking until it has been discussed with someone - anyone!
- He isn't very good at thinking things through on his own and finds talking to himself helpful.

- He's discovered that asking questions out loud often releases answers for him without needing an answer from the person he's talking to.

Just talking it through has really helped
– thank you so much!

- His best friend is an Internal Thinker who gets frustrated with him because Jason will ask for an opinion without seeming to value the answer.

- He often starts conversations with statements like, "I'm not quite sure where I'm going with this yet ...", or, "Let me just bounce some ideas around ..."

125

How to motivate Jason

When struggling, it will not help Jason to give him time to think about things. He needs someone to talk to and doesn't have a helpful internal dialogue.

He may appear to want advice but is actually often just looking for a chance to 'externally process' so won't understand if you get hurt when he doesn't take your advice, or even listen to it! The best thing to do is to understand and simply be that sounding board.

Alison is an inside thinker

- She needs to be given space to think about things.
- She doesn't know how she feels about something until she's given time to think.
- Asking her to give an opinion without giving her that space to think can be quite frustrating for her.
- In a complicated situation she needs some time before she's ready to take on board any consequences
- Her best friend is an *Outside Thinker* who she sometimes finds thoughtless and impulsive.

How to motivate Alison

When she is struggling, Alison will benefit from being given a bit of time. She needs to work through her internal feelings or dialogue before she's ready to deal with any decisions or consequences. It could be easy to interpret her quietness as non-cooperation but this is simply her way of processing the information.

Applying the Inside/Outside thinker filter

The situation:

Having finished the project from Chapter 6 you are given a brand new one, this time to manage right from the start. Your team are ready to respond to your clear leadership.

Inside thinker:

You look through the project brief. It's an interesting challenge and you begin to work through all the different aspects. You know your team reasonably well and so you start to allocate roles within the project. By the time your team briefing is due you've got pretty well everything wrapped up and are ready to tell everyone what's going on...

... Except it doesn't quite work out as well as it did in your head. For some strange reason team members appear strangely resistant to take on the roles you've assigned them. And if that wasn't difficult enough, you find there are irritating small issues that have arisen that weren't on the original brief that people keep throwing in. If only they had told you from the beginning you could have allowed for them but now they keep derailing the process you had so clearly mapped out.

Your strength is the ability to work through something and come out with answers. Your weakness is that you aren't very good at involving others in that process. The truth is that, at some level, you don't really need them. Where it feels like the team are being difficult maybe you need to give them space to voice opinions. Possibly all they need is to feel more involved and consulted in decisions that can have quite an impact on their work. Recognising this in future and deliberately choosing to ask them for input at an early stage may prevent all sorts of frustrations further down the line. Not only may you gain important information, relevant to how ideas will work out in reality, but you will also gain the goodwill and support of the team.

Outside thinker:

You look through the project brief and struggle to see how it's all going to fit together. So, the first thing you do is begin to involve others (or at least that's what they think you're doing).

They are impressed that well before forming any ideas yourself you are asking them for their input. At first this builds a great team spirit, but gradually they begin to notice that you aren't really taking their ideas on board. What is actually happening is that you are using them as a sounding board for your own ideas! As an *Outside Thinker* you need to voice your thoughts, get them outside of your head so you can see and hear them clearly and find out how you feel about them. You don't have that internal dialogue that allows you to do all of that inside your head.

By the time the team briefing comes around you've given the impression, wrongly, that you don't care what they think and are going to do it your way anyway.

The answer is to find ways of externalising your thought processes in safe environments where team members don't feel ignored and where you don't appear indecisive. Having a safe person to talk to, who will just be there and allow you to externally think, is a really valuable asset to cultivate (I don't know where I'd be without mine!) It will also help to learn how to think externally without needing to talk to someone - creating charts, mind maps etc can be a good way of doing this. Finally, it is worth talking to your team and being explicit about how you work and explaining in advance for those times when you sound like you're asking for their opinion while all you're really doing is finding out what yours is!

Chapter 8

Do you want the detail or the overview first?

Why some petty-sounding people could save you a great deal of trouble. And how to avoid driving off a cliff.

Chunk Size filter

People seem to naturally tend towards detail or full picture. They either like to get right in and look at the steps involved in the project, or they want to stand well back and consider the bigger implications and see the whole thing from beginning to end. Some people are good at doing both, some people are only good at one or the other. Many projects have failed because either the project manager never looked up from the detail for long enough to see the whole thing was failing, or because he never cared for the specifics that ultimately derailed the whole thing.

A Detail Person (small chunk) is excellent to have around when you need to deal with facts and figures, where small differences could be the deciding factor between success and failure. They will tend to immerse themselves in a project and can become fixated on getting it 'just right'. Sometimes they can be very skilled at seeing the next step and problem solving. They are happiest when dealing with what they consider the 'real stuff', the actual bits and pieces that make up a process, whether that's physical items or data. They can get lost and demotivated when asked to 'chunk up', to think about the bigger picture. They tend not to be good at setting vision for their teams but preferring to get on and work with someone else's vision.

An Overview Person (big chunk) may be excellent at seeing what needs to be done at a bigger level. They get quickly bored by lots of information and want to know the 'broad brush stokes'. They can often be the dreamers, the people who can generate vision and see the bigger possibilities. They are happiest when not bogged down by minutiae but are able to get on with what they would call the 'real business of leading'. They can get quickly demotivated by having to deal with what they would see as petty issues. They can make great leaders but may lead confidently down a disastrous road because they haven't paid enough attention to the smaller needs of the journey. As they say, *'the devil is in the detail'.*

This filter is a little different in that it is more about **direction** than where on some continuum a person sits most comfortably. So we're talking about whether someone likes to start with the detail and move towards the overview, or start with the overview and gradually chunk down into smaller and smaller pieces.

Small chunk or big chunk – How can you tell?

A good question to use to work out this filter is;

"If you were about to start a new project would you want to see the details or the overview first?" (You may need to make it clear that they can have either at any time, the question is about which they would like to see first). Or you could ask;

> *When you want to evaluate the value of a book do you seek to get a feel for the whole thing first or do you dive in to read a small section to see*

what it's like?

It should be quite obvious when someone likes the detail or the overview. The key here is which they would go to **first.**

Typical Big Chunk Answer:

"I'd want to see what's it's all about first, get a feel of the thing and understand the overall objectives".

Typical Small Chunk Answer:

"I'd want to see how you're intending this to work, what the key factors for success might be"

It's all about whether the objectives and vision take the person's attention, or whether they quickly get involved in details and process issues.

What amazing detail on the ends of your antennae

Tim is a small chunk person

- Tim is happiest when dealing with details
- He tends to be good at spotting small mistakes
- He may be good at trouble shooting and creating ideas for the 'next step forward'
- He is not good at seeing longer term issues that may arise
- He gets frustrated with people who seem to talk in vague terms and don't supply the relevant details to keep something 'grounded'

How to motivate Tim

Make sure he has plenty of information and the tools to manipulate it in whatever way is relevant to the project. For example, it's not particularly helpful to give him a set of figures unless he's able to put them in a spreadsheet and play with the possibilities of making small changes to different parts of the process. Tim probably likes those moments where something fails and needs solving. If there is a blockage somewhere in the process, it might be good to call him in to ask for his ideas. He is likely to enjoy dreaming up a possible solution, try it out and then keep creating new ones until the issue is resolved.

Helpful Language

Tim uses 'solid' words and talks in 'grounded' concepts. He doesn't particularly like metaphors, principles or other such abstract ways of thinking.

Louise is a big chunk person

- Louise loves to explore concepts and ideas
- She is good at abstraction
- She can be quite visionary in her way of looking at a process and seeing possibilities
- She gets quickly frustrated by people who insist on talking about the details and exactly how it's going to work out
- Louise often misses small errors, partly because she doesn't see them as very important and partly because she doesn't stop long enough to notice them
- She's not very good at trouble shooting unless it involves overall direction and outcomes

How to motivate Louise

Allow her to dream. Give her the space to explore outrageous ideas. She almost certainly isn't really suggesting that they would all be good ideas so much as exploring them to find something that would be good. Ask her opinion about the bigger issues and release her where possible from everyday repetitive tasks. Give her roles that provide the opportunity to play with different ways of succeeding

We'll conquer the world with this!.

Helpful Language

Louise likes to talk about the bigger issues and likes concepts. She may use metaphor to try to express the wider issues in her brain. She will tend to work in abstractions or ideas rather than concrete ideas.

Applying the Chunk Size Filter

The situation:

As for Chapter 7 you have been given a new project to deliver. It's not something you've done before and so you're starting from scratch.

Small chunk size:

You grab hold of the project and get stuck in. You love the details and enjoy working out the first steps to take. You're good at seeing the next step and are happy sorting out the details that the team are going to ask for as soon as they get started. By the end you have a really good handle on what needs to be tackled first, who is going to do what and the resources they need to do it. You're confident that everything's in place for that first team meeting. However, it doesn't quite work out like you imagined...

… Some of your team are happy to take on what you've given them and get the project started. But there's a group of them who keep asking questions you haven't got answers for. It sounds like they want to know timings you couldn't possibly know at this stage and they keep asking for grand sounding project outcomes when all you want to do is get started and allow things like that to grow organically as you progress. You end up being far more didactic than you intend simply so that you can get moving. You know that these bigger issues will become obvious as progress is made.

Your strength is in the detail, you are good at seeing what needs to happen next and can be quite creative when it comes to problem solving at this sort of level. However, to successfully manage a project you also need to be able to step back and see the whole thing. You need to be able to grasp the wider goals and the implications of the entire project. Sometimes you can learn to do this although it doesn't come easily. Sometimes you need to involve someone else who can help you comprehend these larger issues. Whichever way you do it, it does need to happen or you can happily lead your team step by step over a cliff edge that you never saw coming because you were so good at helping them to take the next step.

Big chunk size:

Although the project is quite ambitious you love this sort of challenge. You can see the benefits from running the whole project efficiently and look forward to getting started. In preparation for the team briefing to launch the project you amass a range of facts and figures showing the long-term gains to be made by the company and the clients. You spend quite a while pulling together a clear statement that summarises the overall outcomes and also provides an audible logo for the project. You prepare a PowerPoint to share the vision and look forward to the meeting. But it doesn't quite go to plan...

... It all starts fine but you get increasingly annoyed by team members who constantly get distracted by details when you want to share the broad brush strokes. One person even asked about travel details! Honestly, how can we begin to deal with such petty details until we're all clear about where we're going? You get over the many irrelevant questions to finish the presentation but find a large number of the team dissatisfied by the facts and figures. They find it all too vague and want to know more important down-to-earth details like how to arrange holidays around the timescale of the project. You finish quite frustrated by the small-minded group you've been lumbered with. If only they could raise their eyes from the path and look at the landscape!

Your strength is all about big picture. You can plan the direction and overall vision of a project. You know exactly why the project is important and how it fits in with other company initiatives. Your weakness is in the detail. Some of your team will be, almost by definition, *doers* – practical people able to get on and get things done. Some of them will need to know the specific logistics and resources and timings and ... details. You either need to learn to chunk down to this level of specificity or appoint someone who can. Or you may find yourself leading your particular army successfully around the cliff edge you saw coming from a long way back, only to run out of fuel in the middle of the desert.

Chapter 9

What about you?

Working out your next three filters

VAK

One of the easiest ways of getting some idea of your Visual, Auditory or Kinaesthetic preference is to get someone to look at your eyes while they ask the questions listed in Chapter 6 (See Chapter 6 for instructions). This is an interesting hint and suggests your preference. There are several other things you can notice to support, or challenge, this 'diagnosis'.

At the end of Chapter 6 there is a table outlining the dress code, sitting position, pace of speech and even shoe preference of different patterns. Have a look through those and decide where you fit, or even better ask someone else who knows you well to do it for you (You will view yourself through our own filters and that can make it difficult to judge yourself clearly).

145

Remember we are all a mixture of all of these. We don't fit nicely into any box, no matter how well it's crafted.

Inside/Outside Thinker

Imagine you had a new task to tackle. Would you spend time chatting with other people about it, exploring the possibilities **first** (*Outside*)? Or would you spend some time thinking through the issues before you were ready to talk to others about it (*Inside*)?

Do you tend to go quiet when you need to think about something (*Inside*)? Or do you tend to get noisier when you need to think something through (*Outside*)?

Do you find it fairly easy to work out your opinion about something entirely inside your own head, even to the point of considering different options before choosing what you think is the best one (*Inside*)? Or do you find it almost impossible to think something through internally, and if there isn't anyone to talk to about it do you talk to yourself (*Outside*)?

Chunk Size Filter

Do you like to get a broad overview of a project before getting involved in the detail (*Large chunk*)? Or when someone's talking about a project do you find you mind constantly thinking up answers to some of the issues that may arise (*Small chunk*)?

Do you find details annoying and people who obsess about them petty (*Large chunk*)? Or do you find vision strategy and long term goals a distraction from being able to get on with the task at hand (*Small chunk*)?

When making a meal do you focus **first** on the way you want everyone to feel (*Large chunk*)? Or do you tend to think **first** about what you've got in the freezer and what you might need to buy? (*Small chunk*)

Where does your attention naturally go - to the outcomes and the big picture or the details and the next step?

Phase 3

The third set of filters

Options/Procedures Filter

Time Experience Filter

Time Perceptual Filter

Chapter 10

Do you think in straight lines?

Why do some people answer a simple question with a long-winded story?

Options or Procedures Filter

This filter, more than some of the others, is about the way people think through things. Some people like to look at all the options available and make a choice based on some criteria that they consider important. Other people will be confused by lots of choice and would much prefer to work through the issue sequentially.

An *Options* person loves to create possibilities and find new ways of doing something. They can be a little overwhelming in the way that they tackle a project since they will come up with more and more different ways of achieving the same objective. They may not to be very good at finishing off a project since it can be perceived that to finish something will limit the options. However, if they believe that by completing a project they will then be offered a wide range of different opportunities then they will tend to get frustrated by the need to finish off the current project and may even rush it and finish poorly. Maybe it's time to find a procedural person who will finish of the project properly!

A *Procedures* person likes process and structure. They are most comfortable having a bulleted list, or even better a numbered list, to follow. They like to see a clear start and end to a project and can get frustrated when the agreed process is not followed. They tend to be more interested in how to get something done and not too worried about why it's being done. *Procedures* people tend to be good at starting and finishing things (often referred to as a 'completer/finisher'). They like to know where it starts; make that start, work through the steps required and then finish. They tend to be good at following rules because they value those rules. They tend not to be so good at thinking flexibly about a problem.

Options or Procedures – How can you tell?

Ask any question that starts with the word, 'Why' and enquires about a choice they have already made. For example:

> *Why did you choose the job you're doing?*
> *Why do you drive the car you drive?*
> *Why did you choose that place to go to for your holiday?*

You are listening for whether they talk about criteria behind their choice or tell a story?

Typical Options answers:

> *I chose this car because it was the right price, with the specific gadgets I was looking for. I also like the colour and petrol consumption*

> *I'm working in this department because I'm good at accounts, like the team, enjoy the flexible working hours offered and see great opportunities for promotion*

These answers give a set of criteria by which to measure the choice that they made.

Typical Procedures Answers:

> *I bought this car because when we were looking we tried all sorts of different models and makes. Then we came across this garage that had been recommended by a friend. This car was sitting outside and as soon as we came around the corner I knew it was the right one for me. Of course we did all the right things, test driving it, haggling etc but it felt inevitable that our search had ended up right there.*

> *I didn't really choose this job. My previous role was in personnel and when they decided to restructure my role was due for reassessment. I went through the assessment process and it was felt that it would suit my skills and experience to move to accounts*

Procedures people tend to see life in sequential patters and so when asked 'why' will answer with a story rather than criteria. They will substitute the word 'Why?' for 'How?' If asked about 'choice' they will tend to see events as reasonably inevitable with little choice being made.

Wow! So many ideas!

Gloria is an Options Person:

- Gloria likes choice
- She is good at creating possibilities and seeing options where others get stuck
- She is happiest being allowed to explore her own way of doing something
- She may not follow the rules very well - seeing them as guidelines for those with less imagination
- She gets excited when planning new projects but is poor at seeing them through to the end

153

- She is often quite good at juggling projects, keeping several things going at the same time
- She gets frustrated by people who see only one way of doing something or who work sequentially through a list
- Procedures people will find her difficult because she rarely sticks to the point and sees something through to completion
- Gloria may dress slightly unusually, trying out new mixes of clothes

How to motivate Gloria

Gloria works best with space to explore rather than feeling pinned down to a fixed way of doing things. Her creative spark is one of her true talents and if this is smothered she will tend to lose any passion in her role. If she's struggling then the best thing to offer her is the opportunity to find as many ways as possible to make things better. She'll respond much better to that than being given a set of possibilities.

It is worth recognising that her strength does not lie in completing a project and it is best to ask her to do so only if it's absolutely necessary.

Helpful Language

Use words and phrases that create possibility. *"opportunity, unlimited, infinite, chance, release, break the rules, what else, option,"*

Jeff is a Procedures Person:

- Jeff likes to start at the beginning and see it through to the end. He will get frustrated if regularly prevented from finishing things off
- He likes to know where he is in a process and will always be able to tell you 'the next step'
- He likes charts and bullet points and anything that represents where he is in a sequence
- He finds it hard to tune into more abstract issues like how 'he's doing generally' and will answer such questions by relating it back to concrete steps
- He finds Options people difficult because he will be looking for a clear answer and not the various choices that are being offered
- Options people may brand him 'dull' or 'lacking in inspiration'He will work hard to see something completed and may not mind if the task is reasonably repetitive.

Right – now what's next on my check list?

How to motivate Jeff

Jeff thrives in an environment where he knows what has to be done next. If he's finding work hard it's probably because he is unclear about the process, or because he is in a changing environment where what he was going to do next has been changed. To get the best out of Jeff give him plenty of structure; keep things like team meetings to a set day and time each week. Let him know what he's achieved so far and ask him what he's going to do next.

Helpful Language

Use words that create certainty and a sense of
sequence:
*"first, then, last, next, process, the right way,
trusted, what next, finish, start"*

Applying the Options/Procedures Filter

The situation:

Remember that project you were landed with
in Phase 2? It's still relevant and you're
preparing for the team meeting where you're
going to launch it.

Options filter:

You are excited by the opportunities this
project offers. You can see all sorts of ways in
which you and your team are going to be able
to enjoy the whole process. As you look more
closely at the project you notice all sorts of
alternatives within the bounds of the project -
plus there are some amazing possibilities just
outside of the bounds of the project that you're
sure will be OK to include. As you consider all
the possibilities it seems that the sky's the limit!

157

You prepare a ritzy presentation, looking forward to the morning when you can share your exciting ideas with your team. But it doesn't quite go as you expected...

... At first the team seem to be caught up with your excitement. But you are slightly disappointed by Geoff. Early on in your presentation he starts to question how this all fits with company policy. Can't he see past the petty issues of the way it's usually done and grasp all of the possible ways we could handle this? Then others join his blinkered attitude by wanting to know which way was *best*. They even suggest that we ought to follow the proven methodology for this sort of project and begin to pin it down to certain steps. It all felt very disappointing when it should have been such a great start!

Your strength is in looking at a situation and seeing possibilities. You are at your best in fast moving environments, constantly coming up with new ideas to meet the changing conditions. Your weakness is shown up in any situation when policy is paramount, when safety is of particular importance or when getting something done in a set way is more important than flair. Your team may tire of you constantly changing 'the rules' to suit your newest idea. While you love change, they may suffer from change fatigue.

Procedures Filter:

The team meeting is tomorrow and you have set up a wonderfully sharp, precise path through the whole project. You've carefully considered past precedent and company policy and have mapped out the *right way* to tackle what you have been asked to do. You've even been able to create a model of 'Seven Steps to Success', and colour coded each step for clarity. You're looking forward to sharing such a well thought through project. But the team didn't seem to completely share your enthusiasm...

... It all started well with your outline of the project. But they began to get restless when you shared your pathway through the demands. There was a clear loss of heart when Lyn suggested that we did a section a different way. It wasn't that you minded the question but then others started making their own suggestions and it was so hard to get everyone back on track. In the end you got a bit cross with everyone for messing up your 'Seven

Steps' and the meeting finished without that sense of pulling together that you expected.

Your strength is found within a process. You can take an idea and turn it into something doable. By creating a clear pathway with measurable milestones along the way you are able to create momentum towards the end goal. Where you are out of your depth is when things are more flexible and the goalposts move regularly. Because you like to stick to the rules, you assume everyone else will and you can be blindsided by sudden change.

Chapter 11

Do you enjoy doing or watching?

Do you like to be in the middle of the action or prefer to sit back and watch others making fools of themselves?

Time Experience Filter

I spent quite a while pondering on whether to include these two filters about time. They've got a slightly different feel to them and certainly a different application. In the end you are reading them because I have found them profoundly helpful to understand when working with certain people.

Most people can imagine time as something linear, with the past stretching out in one direction and the future stretching out in another, usually opposite, direction.

161

Occasionally people struggle with such simplicity and I've come across all sorts of models, including one woman who could only imagine time as a big blob floating in the air in front of her. However, most people are happy to imagine the line. This filter asks about where you see yourself in relation to that line. It gives a helpful insight into how people handle themselves in various situations.

Before exploring this filter any further, let me describe a time when I used it. I'd been asked to meet the director of a training and consultancy business by a mutual friend who thought we'd both benefit from getting together. We met for lunch at a Beefeater somewhere on the Southern edge of London. After the initial polite conversation we ordered our meals and she turned to me and said, *"So Justin, what is it that you do?"*

I nearly launched into my usual spiel describing some of the types of business situations I support and then stopped, looked across at her and said, *"Tell you what, I'll show you".*

I went on to describe how she handled herself in meetings, her main role, her strengths and her weaknesses. I had no way of knowing such information and so she sat back away from me not sure whether she was entirely comfortable with this weirdo who knew too much. "In for a penny..." I thought to myself and pressed on by describing how she behaved at parties and why her husband found her frustrating on holiday! Fortunately her sense of curiosity overcame her sense of self-preservation and she leaned forward once more and asked some pertinent questions. The key question was, *"How the hell do you know that?"*

I knew all that about her because I'd spotted how she handled time and just made my best guess from that.

To help you discover your own and other people's filter pattern we're going to change things around a bit for these two filters and get you a little more involved.

Read the next few paragraphs carefully, and then follow the instructions.

First, as you sit, stand or lie, imagine you could point to your past. I know that's a strange question but don't get too hung up about it because the answer you give isn't too important at the moment. If you simply can't imagine pointing in a direction to suggest your past then pretend that you can do it and do it

anyway. So pause now and point somewhere....
Done it? Don't read on until you have!

You can put your finger back down for the
moment, but keep it handy. Many people point
directly behind them to indicate their past.
That's common but by no means universal, for
example my line is off to the left.

Now I'm going to ask you to do it again but this
time point to the future. Go ahead, right now,
pick that finger up. Which direction is your
future? ... You should be pointing in some
direction right now. Are you? Remember the
direction and you can relax again for the
moment.

Many people will point straight ahead of them;
that's especially common for those who
pointed at their past as going off behind them.
In my case my future is off to my right.

You should now be able to imagine two lines
representing your past and your future. We
need to do something now that some people
find easy and some more difficult - let's
pretend you're one of those who find it easy
shall we? Take your past line and if it's not

there already drag it around so you can see it. If it was behind you then maybe it's easiest to simply turn sideways on so that you can look down it. Alternatively you can pull it around into view. If possible, the best place to put it is somewhere going off at an angle in front of you. Then we need to do the same to your 'future' line. Drag that one so that you can see it clearly, again preferably off to an angle in front of you. See the diagram below for the ideal place to put these lines.

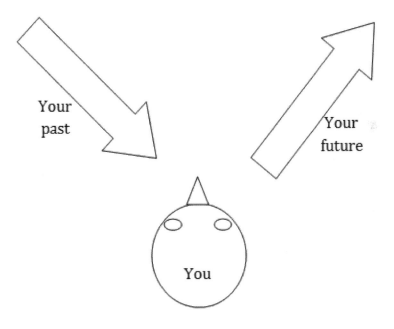

It doesn't matter which side your past or future are, you just need to be able to see them both. Pause in your reading now and see if you can do what I'm suggesting...

... Are you there? Good, well done. Now let's make them a little more real by putting some events on to them. As you look down your past, imagine you can see some events like your last birthday, your earliest memory, the day you got your first car, the first time you.... well, you get the idea. Put four or five things on it to make it a little more real. Then do the same with the future line. Where would tomorrow breakfast go? What about your next birthday? Can you imagine the point on this line where your next milestone birthday might go? Look way, way down and notice where your 70th birthday would go. Stop reading now and give it a try...

... I hope you're still with me. We're nearly there now. Just look up from the book and imagine that line one last time, coming all the way from your past towards you and off into the distance into your future away from you. Do it now. If you've got this far it's worth not skipping this last step.

Right, here's the question we've been building up to for the last few minutes ... that line you saw ... did it go in front of you or through you?

Or to put it another way, the present, the right now moment, is that inside your body or are you looking at it?

A strange exercise finishing in a strange question. Let's now have a look at what your answer tells you.

The line was in front of you

This suggests that you perceive time to be something just slightly removed from your experience. It's almost like you're sitting back and observing life going on. We call this an *'Out of Time'* filter (NLP calls this *'Through time'* which many find a bit confusing). My lunch companion was quite strongly *Out of Time.* Below is a list of the sort of things I told her:

Kath is Out of Time:

- In meetings she tends to sit back and let the others argue
- She's the one who pulls things together at the end

- She's quite good at 'seeing the wood for the trees'
- Kath stays cool in an emergency, reacting appropriately rather than in a panic
- She finds it hard to 'switch off', even on holiday
- People might say of her that she's a little 'cold' which she thinks is quite unfair, she cares deeply about people but just isn't as gushy as some
- At a party she's much happier leaning against the wall watching what's going on than in the middle of the dance floor
- Her strength is that she keeps her cool, her weakness is that she isn't sure how to get hot!

I wonder what the sales figures are doing today.

The line was running through you

This suggests that you perceive time to be something that happens right here and now and you're in the middle of it. We call this 'In Time'. Instead of the slight removal that Kath feels you experience the highs and the lows of life. It may mean that you enjoy life more when things are going well but suffer more when it's not.

Atul is In Time:

Forget tomorrow – I'm enjoying myself now

- In meetings Atul gets involved and argues with the best of them though may lose the point of it all in the immediacy of the discussion
- He can be a bit quick to react and doesn't always think about the consequences
- Atul is known in the office for being fun, though when he's low he does tend to spread that around too
- He finds it easy to switch off and is skilled at immersing himself into whatever environment catches his attention

- At a party he's happier throwing himself in and dancing in the centre than sitting back and watching. If he does feel chilled then he does it full-on.
- His strength is his enthusiasm for the task at hand; his weakness is a lack of awareness for what might happen next

Flexing around the Time Experience Filter:

Like all the filters, learning what you do well is valuable. It allows you to do it even better. Plus, learning how to work within the other filter can give you a number of options. Ones that simply weren't available to you before.

This is just as true with this filter. What's different is that the others usually simply take practice. How can you practice being *In* or *Out of Time?* It turns out there's a simple exercise you can do to learn to handle both patterns. I've taught this to many people and had some great feedback about the results it's brought. Like the process you've just completed it may sound a bit strange, but if you give it a go I suspect you'll enjoy it.

First find yourself a bit of room to stand in. You need space in front and behind you. Now imagine your time lines again. You may need to imagine them back where they were and drag them around or you may find you've already developed the flexibility to put them in front of you straight away. It's helpful to put a few dates on the lines like before to make them that bit more real for you.

Part One:

Visualise the line clearly, either going through you or in front of you.

If you see it in front of you then take a step forwards into the line. Stop there and notice how different it feels to experience time right now. Once you're comfortable in that place take a step back, out of time, so you can see the line in front of you again and notice the different feelings that you feel when you're looking at the moment rather than experiencing it (I did warn you that this was a little strange. Just go for it and see how it feels).

If, on the other hand, you see the line going through you then take a step back out of it. Do that now and spend a while acclimatizing yourself to how it feels to look on, slightly removed from what's happening right now. Once comfortable *Out of Time*, take that step forward and notice the difference. My advice is to do this a few times before moving on to Part Two.

Part Two:

Now I want you to remember an exciting experience from your past. It could be a holiday experience or a party or an interview or the time you threw yourself out of plane. It doesn't matter what the experience is so long as you have quite strong emotions attached to it. Put that event on your timeline and move the line around so that you are at that point in time (I don't know about you but doing that feels quite strange, not unpleasant, just strange!) Now close your eyes and remember everything you can about it - what were you feeling, seeing, hearing, and saying? Try to put yourself back there. Once you're there do the same exercise we did in Part One. Step forwards or backwards and notice how different it feels to be *In* or *Out of Time*. Do this several times until you are comfortable changing your place on the timeline at will.

The theory is that simply trying to imagine yourself in these different positions is growing new synaptic pathways in your brain to handle these new ways of thinking about yourself and your perceptions. Having done these exercises myself I find it noticeably easier to enter into the spirit of the moment as well as sitting back and enjoying watching.

Applying the Time Experience Filter

The situation:

Because of the amazing success you made of the project in Chapter 11 you are promoted (again) and are now responsible for the team you were part of.

In Time:

Aware that you are going to be the driving force behind the new team you spend the weekend getting into the right state, making sure you are rested and in the best state possible. You arrive on your first day thrilled to be there are ready to get going. This is an exciting day and one you are going to wring every bit of pleasure and value from. You know you 'don't get a second chance to make a first impression', so you are particularly focussed on each person you meet, making sure they feel good about having you in this role. You put all your energy into it and the morning goes pretty well, but then people start asking you things you can't answer...

... Gill from accounts wants to know your projected costs. How can you know that until we've had a month to see what happens? Graham from transport pops in to say congratulations, but on his way out reminds you of the need to pre-book all transport needs with him, preferably a month in advance. You laugh at first thinking he's joking but then quickly sober up when you realise he's serious. Then there's Sandra. You've always got on well with Sandra. She's been great fun to have in the team, but even she put you under pressure when she started asking about her future role. Couldn't everyone just get on as normal and give you a chance to enjoy your first day?

Your strength is the ability to throw yourself into a situation, empathising with those involved. People find you personable and fun, often easy to talk to and a good listener. Your weakness is that you can get so immersed in what's going on that you don't stop to consider the implications and longer term view. People can find you frustrating because, while they may like you, they may find you a little shallow.

Out of time:

Aware that many things are going to be asked of you as soon as you start, you spend the weekend predicting where the immediate 'pinch points' are going to be. You arrive on Monday calm and looking ahead to a successful first month. Many people call in to congratulate you and you are especially pleased to have all the figures that Gill and Graham want already to hand. Thank goodness you had the good sense to plan ahead! All is going so well, everything is in place and everyone has what they need to get on. But if you're honest you're a bit disappointed by the lack of enthusiasm...

... The team used to have lots of fun, why are they so different these days? It all feels a bit heavy. Surely everyone appreciates the way you have everything tied down? As the month passes the team are functioning reasonably well and you look set to hit your quarterly targets but there's no sparkle anymore and no chance of winning the high performance team award this time around.

Your strength is in planning and responding thoughtfully to anything thrown at you. If you're creative, it's in a thought-through considered manner. In a crisis you react with clarity and purpose. Not much takes you by surprise and you tend to be well prepared for all meetings. Your strength is also your weakness (as is usually the case). You find it hard to be spontaneous and, unless you take steps to counter it, your team will tend to reflect your fairly serious, slightly removed feel. People are not entirely sure what you're feeling about things because your responses have that slightly measured feel, as though it's been filtered before coming out, which is not a bad description of what's actually going on.

Chapter 12

How do you remember past events?

Are you still living with past mistakes? Do they still cost you something every time you remember them? Or perhaps you know someone like that.

Time Perceptual Filter

This is an easy filter to explore and it can have huge implications for how we feel about things.

We're about to go through a very simple process. It won't take very long. If you follow the instructions and complete the first part without reading on first you are more likely to gain from the process.

Please make sure you're somewhere where you can safely close your eyes and reflect for a moment. We're about to access memories which may feel a little uncomfortable. For this to 'work' it doesn't have to be any major event from your life. It is not worthwhile getting upset, so choose something that was disappointing rather than something devastating.

When you're ready to, think about a time in the past where it went badly for you, some event which you wish had not happened or had worked out differently. Thought of one? In a moment I'm going to ask you to close your eyes and remember the event as clearly as you can. It may help to try to remember how it felt, what you saw, heard and said at the time.

Where exactly are you? What are you wearing? Who is there with you?
Ready? Then close your eyes and visualize it as clearly as you can. When you've got a clear picture then come back, I'll be waiting for you here.

Done it? Got a clear picture? If not then don't read on. Take the 20 seconds it requires.

Once done, here's the important question to ask ... as you looked at the scene could you see yourself? To put it another way, were you looking at it as though through a slightly removed camera lens or were you looking at it through your own eyes? Your answer to this question shows how *associated* to the past event you were.

If you were looking through your own eyes then this suggests that the feelings of sadness/disappointment etc are still feelings that are relevant and meaningful to you today. It shows you still *associate* to that time and haven't let the past be the past. In some part it is still 'present' to you and probably still costs you because of it. That is not the only option; you can change that if you want. We'll explore exactly how to do that in a moment.

People tend to be fairly consistent with the way they handle the past, especially painful memories. It may be worth the short period of time it takes for you to think of other disappointing memories. If you're happy to do it you may want to briefly touch on those really painful memories you carry, just to see what you do with them. Don't stay there too long though will you. The ones where you see through your own eyes are the interesting ones to notice for now.

If, on the other hand, you found yourself seeing the event as through a camera lens with yourself as a subject of the picture then you are more *dissociated* from that event. This tends to mean it hurts you less today because you've found a sense of perspective and emotional distance. For painful memories this is usually a good thing to discover, though for happy memories it may be less helpful. Some people have a pattern of remaining associated to their past; some habitually distance themselves from their past and are more dissociated. Which do you do? What about your colleagues? Your boss? As suggested before, groups can also function with a consistent filter. As a team what do you tend to do; dwell on the past mistakes, feeling the shame, or sweep them aside and move on?

Some of these memories may be of things that happened a long time ago and some very recent. The following technique for giving you an option about how you remember them is both easy and effective regardless of the time span we're talking about. If you did the timeline exercise from the previous chapter then what we're about to do will feel similar. To do this you need to find a safe space where you can stand or sit where you won't be interrupted or feel awkward about being watched.

If you have a painful memory that you'd like to feel free of then this exercise is for you. If there's a happy one you'd like to experience again then we'll do that in a moment. Decide which one right now. If it was a series of events choose one moment that represents the whole experience. When you've chosen bring it back to mind with as much clarity as before and see it through your own eyes once more. Again, it may help to think about who you were with, what you were feeling, saying, doing and hearing. Once you have that clear picture, make it a still shot (i.e. not a movie) and pull back from your own eyes, as though you were operating a very clever camera, and view the scene with you standing in the middle of it. You can pull back as far as you like but try to find a place far away enough so it all feels a bit distant while still close enough to at least see the main people involved. Now look at the scene with this new perspective of someone interested in what's going on but with no emotions vested in it. You're curious about what's happening but not involved. Freeze this new scene and choose to make this your core memory of what happened that day.

Open your eyes and look around. Move your body in some way, perhaps by shaking your arms, going to make a drink or simply sitting in a new seat. When you're happy that you've let go the image and you're properly back in the present then we're ready for the last step. Close your eyes and remember the event again but this time be careful to go back to that last picture - the one where you were looking through a camera lens. Revisit it briefly and then return to the present. If that didn't feel completely natural and you had any sense of fighting with the *associated* picture then do it again until this is the way you recall that event. This simple technique will not only take the sting out of this memory but is giving your mind the skills to do it with other memories. Try it; see how you recall other painful memories. If they are associated, then quickly pull back each time and 'fix' them as dissociated pictures. You'll find it easier this time.

If there are some happy memories that you'd like to have a positive impact on your current life, then the opposite procedure works just as well. Simply go back to the scene but this time seeing it as though through a camera lens. Once you have it clearly pictured then allow the camera to sweep forward, into *your* head and view the scene through your own eyes. Once there, make it a movie rather than a still picture. It may help by making it more colourful and add in a happy sound track running in the background. Feel those same feelings of fun/joy/excitement that you did when you experienced it for the first time. As before, once back in the room, move in some way to let the picture go and then go back, but this time straight into the associated viewpoint and enjoy it all over again. Now try that for other memories; you'll find it easier to do once you've done it the first time.

Of course, I'm not suggesting that all painful memories can disappear in one go. But you might be surprised by how differently you feel about them once you've gone through this process.

Applying the Time Perceptual Filter

The situation:

You're starting your new role as team leader exactly as above.

Associated:

You love your new role and judging by people's responses you are doing reasonably well. It's funny to look back with gratitude on those mistakes you made last year - I bet you never thought you'd be thankful for those embarrassing moments! Every day you re-live that particular debacle and you know that you are NEVER going to make that mistake again! Isn't it funny how we seem to learn more from our failures than our successes?...

...However, there is a shadow side to this too. You are determined not to find yourself in that position again. Just remembering it now makes your face feel hot and you tend to be a little overcautious at times, triple-checking something rather than just getting on with the next thing. Your team notice that you're a little oversensitive about those past mistakes and completely lost your rag with Phil when he'd only made a small error which would have been picked up later anyway. There are times when your team feel like they are walking on egg-shells around certain areas.

Your strength is in learning from the past and not making the same mistake twice. Your weakness is that you find it hard to move on from mistakes and you carry the shame/ pain/ embarrassment/ anger/ disappointment etc with you all the time. This makes you great at avoiding similar situations but rather touchy and difficult to work with when there's the danger that the situation might be repeated.

Dissociated:

You throw yourself into your new role, pleased to have the chance to shine. People seem to be responding well to your new leadership when it all comes crashing down. You can't believe it's happened AGAIN. You feel so unlucky. Lightening isn't supposed to hit twice and it seems pre-ordained that you are going to face this same situation wherever you go. You complain about how unlucky you are and press on, determined to put it behind you and carry on regardless.

Your strength is in being able to continue and not be crippled by events that would make many resign in despair. This is a major strength and must not be underestimated. However, your weakness is that you may not be good at learning from the past and so may find exactly the same mistakes happening again (and again).

187

Chapter 13

What about you?

Working out your last three filters

These three filters are much harder to discern on your own and the best way to learn your patterns is to ask someone to use the questions or processes listed in Chapters 10, 11 and 12 and notice what comes to mind when you answer them.

Options and Procedures filter

If you don't have anyone to ask you the questions then ask yourself why you chose your present job (or car, or home, or partner). This works best if you slow the process down a little, so you either need to answer aloud or write it down. Do it now before reading on.

OK, now look back on your answer; did you talk or write about your various criteria for making that choice? (E.g. *I chose this job because it was close to home, I had the right experience, I liked the company ethical stance and it was the right pay scale*). Or did you tell a story of how you came to choose the job? (e.g. *I had been in my previous role for a number of years and was beginning to get bored when I noticed that this company were advertising for someone of my experience and ...*) If your answer was a mixture of the two, (i.e. you told a story with a range of criteria embedded in it) then you probably belong somewhere in the middle.

If you gave criteria you are showing an **Options** pattern. If you told a story you are showing a **Procedures** pattern. Remember, neither is *better* and both are important in different situations.

Time Experience Filter (In Time or Out of Time)

One way to tell whether you use an 'In time' or 'Out of time' pattern is to look through the descriptions of the two people in Chapter 11 – Kath and Atul – and decide who you are most like. Or, possibly more useful, show them to someone who knows you well and ask them who you're most like. You can also get clues by answering the following questions:

Do you like standing back and watching (*Out of time*) or getting involved (*In time*)?
Do you find yourself able to respond coolly in a crisis (*Out*) or do you respond emotionally (*In*)?
Do you like to think of yourself as a good observer (*Out*) or as a good practitioner (*In*)?
Do you prefer to dance (*In*) or watch (*Out*)?

Time Perceptual Filter (Associated or Dissociated)

Again the simplest way of learning your pattern is to go through the process outlined in Chapter 12. However, you may also find some hints contained in your answers to these questions:

Does it hurt you to remember painful times from your past? (*Associated*) Or are you quite phlegmatic about past mistakes? (*Dissociated*)
Do you dwell on things, reliving them and wishing you had done them differently? (*Associated*) Or are you comfortable telling others about your mistakes because they are in the past and so no longer really relevant?

(*Dissociated*)

Can you remember every detail of an embarrassing moment? (*Associated*) Or do you only remember the general storyline? (*Dissociated*)

Phase 4
Going Deeper

VAK – taking it further

Filters working together

Evolution not Revolution

Chapter 14

VAK

Seeing further, hearing the subtleties and going deeper

Responding in the moment

We've said before that people are too complicated to fit in a box. It's easy, and very tempting, to say someone is a 'visual person' and leave it at that. This statement is **always** wrong. No matter how visually orientated an individual; they are **always** more than that as well. Like all the filters being discussed in this book this one is a helpful concept rather than a clearly defined 'rule'. However, because there is an easy-to-spot visual clue as to what's going on inside their head, we can respond immediately to what we see happening.

Once you become aware of the way people's eyes move you can begin to notice it all the time. You will become able to react in the moment to what you see. So when someone who normally looks up changes and looks down when thinking about something try asking:

What are you feeling right now about this?

Or maybe, if you notice someone who habitually looks to the side looks up when thinking about the question you just posed, you could try asking:

What is it that you're seeing right now?

The same works for someone who looks to the side, you could ask:

What are you telling yourself?

The nice thing about these questions is that they can appear perfectly normal within the conversation and so there's little risk of breaking rapport or looking stupid while trying these out.

Are they lying?

Telling whether someone is lying is a very complicated issue. There are many small signs to watch out for but it takes years of practice to be good at spotting them and even then it's still very much an art not a science. So when people tell you they can always tell when someone lies, it's a pretty safe bet that they have just lied. And even here it's not that simple, they might really think they are able to tell, so they are not lying, just self-deceived.

However, one of the interesting signs to watch out for is to notice the side that people look to when they remember information. For example, one of my team usually looks up (*visual)* to remember things. But it's not just 'up', it's usually up and to the left. So her memory space is there - up and to the left. When she thinks about something and looks up and to the right she's not accessing memory, she's accessing her imagination. So when she looks up and to the right before saying something I know that at least in part she's probably imagining something rather than remembering it. That doesn't necessarily equate to 'lying', it may be that she's trying to give the answer that she thinks I want, but it does suggest that the answer isn't a clean representation of what happened.

I was working in an organisation where a very needy employee was accused of something. He confessed to it because he thought that is what the slightly scary manager wanted and what he thought would make the angry people happy. I noticed that his eye movements didn't follow his normal pattern which suggested to me that he was trying to say the right thing as opposed to saying what happened. I stepped in and asked for more details of the actual event and he didn't have them. He hadn't done what he confessed to; he just thought that this would make everyone happy.

This process often catches people's imagination and it appears every now and then in the popular press at the same sort of level as an 'urban myth'. A little while ago someone was 'caught' in CSI because they 'looked the wrong way' when answering questions. Please hear the two important reservations I have about this. Firstly, you have to know which way they normally look before making any assessment. Don't listen to those who say looking right means one thing and left the other. In my experience people can be either, in exactly the same way they might be left or right handed. So just like in a film where they are using a lie detector machine you need to ask a 'baseline question' first (one which will find out which is their normal direction for memory). That means you need to be very confident that they are accessing their memory to answer it. My second reservation goes back to what we've already said, people are very complicated. So once more I encourage you to not take any information you think you gain from this process too seriously!

Patterns of thought

If you get to like all of this you can take it another step further. Most people have a whole sequence of habitual thought patterns, often shown best when they deal with decisions. For example, one senior manager I worked with answered every question by looking up to the left (*visual memory*), then back at me, then off to the right hand side *(auditory imagination)* and then back to me and then answered the question. She did this same pattern every single time I asked her something. What could I deduce from this? I suspected that she felt she had to be very careful what she said in case it was taken wrongly. In fact I got slightly pushier and asked if there had been a time when a casual comment had been misinterpreted causing problems for her in the past. She gasped and said, *"How on earth do you know that?"*

How did I know that? Her memory was on her left side (she looked up to the left to remember the event I'd just asked about) but before answering she played out how the answer would sound in her head before trusting herself to say it (looking into her right hand side - auditory imagination). I'm not saying everyone has such explicit and habitual patterns. I am saying that if you start to look out for them you might be surprised by what you see.

What if you learned that a client had a pattern before making a decision to buy something? For example he might look down, back at you, up to his imagination side, a quick glance to the side before responding to an invitation to buy. His pattern then might be to firstly get a feeling for the purchase (does it feel right?), then to imagine himself owning it (how does it look?) and then using his auditory imagination he is finally deciding what to say to get the best deal. Now you know this you can work with the client through the process. Early on in the pitch you ask questions about how he feels about the item. You then lead him through picturing himself using it before you ask him more auditory questions. Or you can simply go for it in one!

So John, are you feeling good about buying this now? I bet you can imagine yourself back at work using this. So what do you want to say to this offer?

The great thing about this is that if it works you've smoothed the road towards your objective. If it doesn't work, if you've misread the signs or 'John' is simply more complicated than this, then you haven't really lost anything by trying.

Chapter 15

Frame of Reference and Inside/Outside Thinking Filters working together

Whenever I train people to use these filters there is a type of question that always arises. I can almost judge how well a group is handling the new concepts by when this question is asked. It usually involves different specifics but always includes looking for links between the different filters.

The question may involve gender - *"Do you find more women are Outside Thinkers?"* It often tries to link VAK with another filter - *"Are kinaesthetic people more likely to be small chunk?"* Sometimes the question makes a link that is fascinating to explore, though often without any grounding in reality - *"Towards people must also have an external frame of reference, mustn't they?"*

I love these questions because they always reveal the filters of the questioner. I hate these questions because I'm never quite sure how to answer them. There are so many links that seem on the surface to make sense but there is so little research behind them to be able to answer clearly. One way to tackle them is to explore the impact that combinations of filters will have. I suspect this is the subject for another book because there is so much that could be investigated. However, let's explore one such combination together now.

What are the implications of the different patterns created when you combine inside/outside processor and internal/external frame of reference?

There are two ways of benefitting from the exploration of these traits. You can think of yourself and notice the impact that your combination has on your communication styles - where you are strong and weak. Or you can think about someone else (partner, colleague, line manager, boss, spouse!) and recognise the impact that their combination makes on their work and leadership etc.

The table below outlines the main strengths and weaknesses associated with each combination of filters:

	Possible Strengths	Possible Weaknesses
Internal Frame of Reference + Inside Thinker	Able to work alone. Good at making judgements and then taking action on them.	If making a poor decision it may be a while before it comes to light. Can feel strongly about an issue but not communicate this to the rest of the team
Internal Frame of Reference + Outside Thinker	Can make decisions without needing support but includes other people in the process anyway.	Sounds like they're asking for your opinion when they're actually just processing their own thoughts. This can lead to frustration that they don't listen after asking for advice.

External Frame of Reference + Inside Thinker	Can be good at listening to people's comments and criticism, taking it on board and then choosing appropriate responses.	If they don't handle criticism well then they can dwell on small comments and allow them to fester without others being aware that this is happening.
External Frame of Reference + Outside Thinker	Tends to be gregarious, sensitive to other people and eager to talk through any issue to make sure everyone is happy with the process.	Can be a bit overwhelming. Always needing to talk about everything, never just making a decision and getting on with it. Can appear insecure.

Can you recognise yourself here? What about others around you?

You

Look through the list at **your** strengths and weaknesses.
How could you play more to your strengths and downplay your weaknesses?

Who do you work with who could help to cover the areas exposed by your weaknesses?

What would need to happen to enable you to **only** use your strengths?

Your boss

What weaknesses do you recognise in your boss' filter mixture?
How could you make yourself indispensible by covering those weaknesses?

What strengths could you align yourself with and benefit from the 'halo effect' of being involved?

Your direct reports

Go through each of your team and work out their filter combination. If you're not sure, then maybe it would be helpful to ask them some of the questions from the relevant chapters (Chapters 3 & 7).

Now work out where they will shine and where they need support. What does this tell you about where you can support and where you need to be 'hands off'?

It may help you to fill in the chart on the next page.

Who?	Strengths	Weaknesses	Action*
You			
Your boss			
Your team			

*What simple action can you take to make the most of the strengths and minimise the weaknesses?

Chapter 16

Evolution not Revolution

How to introduce any change any time

The 'Relationship Filter' (Chapter 4) introduced the idea that people sort for Similarities or Differences. There are some important implications that this filter teaches us when it comes to sharing information, especially information about change.

Around 5-10% of the adult population are strongly similarities based.

Around 55-65% notice similarities before going on to notice some differences.

Around 20-25% notice differences first and then see similarities.

Around 5-10% is strongly differences based.

As you study those figures they tell you that the vast majority of the population are more comfortable with similarities than differences (Around 70%). Plus another 20-25% is still happy with a focus on similarities even if they don't normally start there. This means that when we have something to share with a group of people it is much better to start from a place of similarities. We need to start with the known, with the safe, with the familiar and only once that's clearly established begin to introduce the new.

Personally, with a strong *Differences* pattern (I'm one of the 5-10%) I love it when I'm offered something new. The very best way to get my attention is to start with a phrase like:

> *This is something completely new, different to everything you've seen before. It's going to change the way you work and the way you think about work. In fact, nothing is going to ever be the same again!*

Now you've got my full attention! I would be on the edge of my seat, dribbling slightly, waiting to get started. This is not normal. Most people are uncomfortable with change, many disliking it, some fearing it. So to start with the new is not the best way to get their attention.

An oft repeated story (possibly only myth) which illustrates this point is told of the move from typing to desktop publishing. It goes like this:

> *You know the old typing pools? Rooms filled with typewriters where people, mostly women, sat every day typing up minutes of meetings, invoices, letters etc. Their role was very predictable with very little variation from day to day. Some of the typists may well have spent their entire working life in the same room doing much the same job. They would have to have reasonably strong Similarities patterns to be able to continue like this, otherwise they would have moved on leaving space for another to fill who had a stronger Similarities pattern.*
>
> *Then, one day, some people arrived with some amazing news.*
> *"Everything is going to change!" they said.*
> *"We've got this amazing new invention that is going to revolutionise your lives. It's called a computer. We're going to*

throw away these old fashioned
typewriters and give you this wonderful
new gadget called a Computer. From
here on life gets better!'"

Can you guess what happened next? The
reaction of these Similarities people was
overwhelmingly to quit. They simply did
not want to embrace the 'wonderful
opportunity' that was being offered.

The computer people learned. They
moved on to the next typing pool due to
be updated with a brand new pitch.

"We've got something to show you," they
said. "Don't worry it's not a big deal.
You're still going to be carrying on as
normal. You'll be sitting here, next to the
same people, doing the same work. Look,
the new machine keyboards have
exactly the same layout as you're used
to. The only difference is that instead of
it printing immediately you get to see it
on the screen first and then it prints.
Otherwise it's all the same".

Can you guess what happened next? The
typists loved the small improvements
being made to their work!

213

Whether this story is based in fact or came originally from an enthusiastic trainer wanting to make his point, it is a good illustration of saying the same thing with a different focus. The computer people in the story almost certainly had a strong Differences pattern, that's why they were on the front edge of technology. They thrived in a Differences environment. However, to be effective in their communication it wasn't what was important to *them* that was important. It was what was important to the receiver of the message being shared that was important! Therefore they had to learn to say it in a way that could be received.

The principle here is, 'Start with the similarities'. Or as a colleague helpfully put it recently, 'Evolution not Revolution'.

From now on, whenever you have something new to share, find a way of sharing what's the same before going on to what is new.

Introducing a new project:

Outline first how it relates to what has gone before. Even if it is completely new to your team there will be elements that they have dealt with before.

Thanks for coming. It's always good to get together like this, like we always do, when we've got something to explore together. Remember when we started that last project? Remember that first meeting? This is the same opportunity for you to get an overview and ask questions. Although we're moving on to something new let me reassure you that we're going to be carrying on as a team. Your roles may appear to be changing but as we stand back and look at this project you can see that you're going to be able to use all the experience you've already built up, because the specific skills you learned in the last project are going to be important in your success in this new one ....

Meeting a new client:

Even if one of your selling points is that you offer something new and different it is still worth spending time making sure that they feel safe (Unless you discern that they have a strong Differences pattern of course!).

As usual, for these sorts of meetings we're going to start by looking at the benefits that changing to our system will give you. We've been in this business for a number of years, with wide experience of dealing with people in your sort of situation. We've often handled your sort of challenges and are used to dealing with your particular requirements. In addition to all of the benefits you have been used to from your previous supplier, we will also bring ....

Introductory meeting with a new coachee/ employee/ direct report:

Usually people appointed to new positions are concerned about all the new things they need to quickly get their head around. It is common practice, and rather unhelpful, for the new manager to want to impress with the new all things coming their way. In an eagerness to emphasise how much better everything is now they've joined, the team the manager may make it harder for that person. It will help them to relax and begin to function efficiently if they are taken from a place of similarity rather than difference.

Welcome. Based on where you've come from I think you're going to like it here. You'll see that we've got the same sense of mission/ fun/ mutual support/ view from the window (Anything you can think of that's the same as where they've come from) as you've been used to. You'll be pleased to notice that all the settings on your computer have carried across and your home access will be essentially the same. Actually haven't we got the same colour walls/ furniture/ carpet/ coffee machine as your previous office?

As well as all the normal stuff, weekly team meetings, daily email checks etc we do a few things differently ...

Sometimes all it takes is a few carefully considered words of sameness to win over otherwise cautious colleagues. 'Evolution not Revolution' is a great rule of thumb.

However, as you talk, you may notice that the person is switched off and not really engaged with you. Then it might be worth trying to emphasise the differences and see if this changes!

Chapter 17

A Filter Interview

How to take someone through all nine filters in one sitting

Sometimes it is helpful to quickly get a measure of someone's filters in one go. This can be done in less than 10 minutes by conducting an interview. These interviews are usually great fun and informative when conducted in the right way and in a good environment. There are a few things to be careful of:

- There are laws about using profiling to support an interview process. This 'interview' is not created for that purpose and should not be used in that situation.
- The concept of a 'profile' is often not helpful since people tend to use it to refer to *nature* rather than *behaviour.* Always remember that these filters are about behaviour rather than character. As such there is plenty of room for

people to change. Remember, *"We don't belong in boxes, no matter how cleverly the boxes have been created".*

- As explained in Chapter 3, sometimes the interviewee gives unexpected answers and the temptation is to spend time digging deeper and deeper trying to find an answer that makes sense. Usually all this does is keep the conversation going until the questioner hears the filter they are looking for. Research has repeatedly shown that the longer someone takes to ascertain the filter, the more likely they are to decide that the person matches their own filter. It's better to leave that question and go on to something you do understand. The metaphor I used in the introduction is helpful here. It's a bit like a meal where you come across a bone. You could spend a long time chewing on the bone trying to digest it when actually there's the rest of the meal waiting to be eaten. It's better to move on and leave the bone on the side of the plate for now. You can always come back to it later if you haven't been filled by the rest of the meal! As a rule of thumb, if you take longer than 10 minutes to conduct the entire interview you're getting too bogged down.

- Look out for the strong filters, the obvious ones. Understanding these will make the biggest difference. Where someone is more balanced it makes less difference to become aware.
- Share the insights the interview has given at the end rather than after each question.
- I am always very open about what's going on and discuss the results with the interviewee. Sometimes I work with young children and I will still chat through the things I notice. I don't like the idea of this being secret information.

Having shared those concerns, the actual interview is very simple to conduct. All you have to do is pay close attention to what they say, being careful not to filter it in any way, otherwise you're simply holding up a mirror and seeing yourself rather than them. The following questions are a simplified form of the questions in each chapter. It may be worth referring to the relevant chapter if you are not clear about the wording below.

One last word of advice about this; have a pen and paper with you. Most people can't hold all the information in their heads, even if they think they can when they begin. It's worth telling the interviewee that you're going to take notes to give good feedback at the end. Once completed, I nearly always give the person the notes so that they have a record of it all. As well as being helpful, it also makes it very clear that I haven't kept a written record of what we've learned.

(1) Direction Filter

> *What do you look for from a job?*
> (Or can ask about *friendship* or *holiday* or *car* etc).
> Get three answers.

> *Why is (that)* important to you?*

Insert into the question the very word(s) they used. Be careful not to change them at all. Do this for all three answers you got from the first part of this question.

Listen for whether they talk about what they **want** or what they **don't want.**

(2) Frame of Reference filter

How do you know when you've done a good job?

Listen for whether they talk about what they **just know internally,** or what they get **from others,** or a mixture of the two. If a mixture, notice which they say **first** since that will be more important for that person.

If **Internal** they often point towards themselves. If **External** they often make open handed gestures including others.

A nice follow up question is,

"Where do you feel that?"

 Internal patterns will point to somewhere on their body (heart, head, stomach). **External** patterns simply don't understand the question.

(3) Relationship Filter

Compare this year to last year.

Similarities will talk about what's stayed the same. **Differences** will talk about what has changed. Or...

Choose two objects that are quite similar with some differences (for example I often choose two similar ballpoint pens) and say to them,

"Tell me about these two objects".

Do they talk about the similarities or differences? If both, which do they notice first?

(4) VAK Filter

Tell me about last Christmas.
(Or your last holiday, or birthday)

Watch their eyes. Do they look up, sideways or down to remember? If they simply look straight at you and answer then make the question harder, e.g. '*Tell me about last Boxing Day',* or, '*Tell me about lunch on the day after Boxing Day'.*

Avoid questions that may automatically focus them on the visual, auditory or kinaesthetic experience. For example,

"Tell me about the concert you went to last week,"

is a poor question since it may focus on the auditory memory.

Also look at the way they are sat, the pace with which they answer, the tone of their voice and how they look (clothes, shoes, shaven, hair brushed etc).

(5) Inside/Outside Processor

When you have a decision to make do you tend to talk about the options with other people first or do you tend to think it through before you involve other people?

What they want to do **first** is the main clue. If they aren't clear or aren't sure then talk about a specific example, e.g.

When you bought your new car did you think through what you wanted before asking for advice or did you start off by chatting with other people to see what they thought before beginning to decide?

(6) Chunk Size Filter

If you were to start a new project would you be most interested in the details or the overview?

Sometimes it's hard for people to know how to answer this and so you can help by holding out your hands and asking them to imagine that in one hand you're holding the broad vision for the project and in the other a plan for how to achieve it - which would they most like to see? Watch the eyes on this one. Their gaze to one hand or the other may tell you more about what they want than their verbal answer does.

(7) Options/Procedures Filter

Why did you choose this job?
(Or can ask, 'Why did you choose to live here?'
Or, 'Why did you choose this car?' Etc).

Options pattern people will answer by giving a set of criteria. **Procedures** pattern people will answer by telling you the story of how they made that choice. Note: some can do both in one answer and so belong somewhere in the middle of the spectrum.

(8) Time Perceptual Filter

Imagine you could point to your past, which direction would you point?
Now imagine you could point to your future, which direction would you point?
You may need to move the lines so that you can see them both (See Chapter 15 for more information)
Draw a line from your past into your future (It may help them to do so with their finger rather than just in their imagination).
Does that line go through you, or in front of you?

In time pattern draws the line going through a part of their body. **Out of time** pattern draws it in front of them.

(9) Time Experience Filter

Close your eyes and remember a time from your past when it all went wrong. Don't worry; I'm not going to ask you to tell me about it.
Remember it as clearly as you can. What did you see, hear, say, feel? Make it a still picture rather than a movie.

Are in you in the picture (i.e. you can see yourself) or are you seeing it as through your own eyes?

Associated see it through their own eyes.
Dissociated see it as through a camera lens and they are in the picture.

It may be worth asking to do this again about a different memory to check consistency before telling them what you're looking for.

Chapter 18

What next?

Where do you go from here? How to begin to use these filters in everyday life.

Well done! You may be surprised how many people don't ever finish a book.

Now you have the tools and the knowledge to do three things:

(1) **Play to your strengths** - you know more clearly what you are good at. Enjoy it. Make the most of your strengths by using them with confidence and choosing work that your strengths are suited to when there is a choice to be made.

(2) **Reduce the impact of your weaknesses -** where possible find someone else to do what you now know you're not very good at. As it happens just this morning my wife turned to me and pointed out something work-based that I've not been very good at getting on with - one of my weaknesses - and offered to take it on and do it for me. Result!

(3) **Be a better leader, manager, coach or team player** by learning how to flex into other people's styles. You'll probably never be *good* at that filter but you can involve people much better by learning to include their styles. The only way I know to do this effectively is to practice. Trying to say it different ways in the car as you drive is a good opportunity for practising (anyone who notices will think you're on the phone).

Remember, none of these filters is intrinsically *better* than or *worse* than the other. They are simply more appropriate or helpful in different contexts. Remember too that you will automatically favour your own set of filters over different ones. You almost can't help doing so. Therefore deliberately value those who are different to you. You need them.

My final piece of advice? Use them! What a shame to invest the time to read this book and then move on to the next thing without putting the learning into practice. A very good way of getting going without being overwhelmed by how much you're trying to pay attention to is to start simply with one filter. Why don't you choose one filter you feel you understand well? Spend the rest of the week looking out for examples of people who filter the same way as you and those who are completely different to you. Watching TV is one great place to look for filters without people thinking you've gone a bit weird! If it's possible, interact with those who are different; try saying things that will appeal to *their* filter and see if they react any differently to you than they normally do. Once you are confident that you understand one filter and can begin to spot it in everyday life then try another one, and then another. You'll surprise yourself just how easy it becomes to both notice them and to begin to unconsciously respond, adapting what you say and do around what people need from you.

The day you catch yourself doing it without meaning to is a good day!

Also by Justin:

Understanding Edward
What your child is actually thinking and what to do about it

If you have children or are a teacher and have enjoyed this book then its accompanying title 'Understanding Edward' will interest you. The book includes much of the same content with examples and applications for dealing with children from around 5 years old to teenagers.

"By explaining the filters you have resolved our biggest problem. We were poles apart on almost every scale. No wonder we couldn't communicate well. We saw almost everything

from a totally different perspective.

Now Sam and I can really talk. We get on better than ever before and have a closer relationship than I had ever imagined.

Words can't express how much you've helped us.

I hope you can bring this experience to every parent, teacher and child alike".

(Excerpt of a letter from a parent after working with Justin)

Available on Amazon.

Graham Shaw – drew the cartoons for this book

Graham is an international conference presenter and trainer specializing in advanced communication and learning skills. He is perhaps best known for his use of fast cartoon drawings during his training. He also runs highly popular programmes that teach people how to use cartoons to make ideas memorable. He also has a very successful e-learning version of the course available on CD-ROM.

Web: www.grahamshaw.net
Email: graham@visionlearning.co.uk

Tel: +44 (0) 1932 253235

Other books from the Kaizen Team:

The trainer's toolkit – bringing brain-friendly learning to life
by Kimberley Hare and Larry Reynolds

"This splendid collection of tools and ideas for trainers draws from the widest variety of sources. It not only gives a useful foundation for applying accelerated learning in the training room, it is also highly practical. We've been waiting a long time for someone to produce such a useful guide - three cheers for Kim and Larry for having finally done some justice to this fascinating and vital topic."
Dr Mark McKergow, international learning consultant and author of The Solutions Focus

Football: Raise your mental game

By Richard Nugent

Football coaches and players at all levels are increasingly having to look elsewhere for that 'psychological edge' - the mental discipline of the game is the fastest growing aspect in football coaching. Football - Raise Your Mental Game takes principles from a number of areas of psychology and applies them to football in an easy-to-read, accessible way. Aimed primarily at players but also invaluable to coaches who wish to use the techniques in a team training environment, it includes chapters on self-confidence, keeping focussed and performing consistently, getting motivated for matches, managing anger, relaxation and dealing with nerves, and positive mental practice. With many testimonies and case studies from professional players and coaches in the game, Football - Raise Your Mental Game is a unique resource for this crucial aspect of football.